QUIRKY HISTORY

*To Jo-anne, my wife and life support system,
and every one of my wonderful family.*

And yes, that includes you, Mimi.*

*See Chapter 15 for how she got her name.

QUIRKY HISTORY

Maritime moments most history books don't mention

JOHN QUIRK

FERNHURST

BOOKS

Other Books by John Quirk

As J Alan Williams

Author
The Kids & Grown Ups Toymaking Book
The Interplanetary Toymaking Book

Illustrator
How to get from January Through December
in Powerboating

As John Quirk

Author & Illustrator
Foul Bottoms

Illustrator
The Sailor's Bluffing Bible
Skipper v Crew; Crew v Skipper
Better Boating Blunders

Published in 2022 by Fernhurst Books Limited
The Windmill, Mill Lane, Harbury, Leamington Spa, Warwickshire. CV33 9HP, UK
Tel: +44 (0) 1926 337488 | www.fernhurstbooks.com

A catalogue record for this book is available from the British Library
ISBN 978-1-912621-42-2

Designed by Daniel Stephen
Printed in India by Replika Press Pvt. Ltd.

CONTENTS

INTRODUCTION

I had the good fortune to go to school in a smoke-blackened relic of the Victorian era in a grubby end of Birmingham. Despite the surroundings, many of the teachers were exceptional. The History, English and Art teachers, in particular, gave me an enthusiasm for these subjects which continue to this day. So you can definitely blame them for this book.

As a ten-year-old I dreamt of playing Stewart Granger

History was not a string of dates but delivered as an on-going drama of events shaped by the personalities of those involved. It was as if we were being told about an adventure film that the masters had just seen. And it was delivered with wit and humour which made it more memorable and entertaining.

The Art master, who left to be the secretary of the British Amateur Racing Drivers Club, drove a string of exciting open sports cars and me into pursuing a career in architecture. I have been eternally grateful for this as it allowed me to draw for a living while travelling the world on interesting and challenging projects. It didn't feel like work. Most importantly, that was how I met my wife when she was a client.

As a ten-year-old, I was captivated to see how dashing Stewart Granger looked in the 1950 *King Solomon's Mines* and vowed that one day I would go to east Africa and play at being him. 14 years later, I left my job as a draftsman in a Birmingham rubber factory, got myself out there and, amazingly, wound up building game lodges in the bush. From there I was asked to join an international hotel group based in New York City and for eight years travelled the world for them before discovering Australia and moving here.

There are critical dimensions in game lodge design; for example, the grabbing distance of an elephant on hind legs and a stupid tourist with a bun is 7.1 metres

All the time, there was this passion for messing about in boats starting with my father's motor cruisers on the River Severn, then out to sea and exploring the south coast and Channel Islands. I built and restored boats in the UK, Kenya and New York and enjoyed a 25-foot sloop on Long Island Sound. The waters and the weather around Sydney are made for boats and the passion continues. We now live in an active fishing village with just over 200 souls. The beach is at the bottom of the garden.

I hope you enjoy reading this as much as I have in putting it together.

Quirky
Patonga Creek
New South Wales, Australia

CAMEL CORPS CAPTURES U-BOAT

The U-boat is still there on the Somalian beach

This chapter title sounds like an extract from the Goon Show's Major Bloodnok's war diaries. "So there I was, laundering my white flag in a wadi when my faithful bearer approached with the news that I was out of clean jodhpurs and there was a U-boat over the next sand dune..."

"And there I was laundering my white flag..."

Except that it is true.

Maybe not the bit about the jodhpurs but astonishingly in 1944 a German U-boat was captured by the Somali Camel Corps. I had heard rumours of this over 60 years ago, but it was thought to be in World War One and it was surrendering to the Turks. I am indebted to Kenya historian Tom Lawrence in the excellent *Old Africa Magazine* who told the story in amazing detail

In 1944, U-852 was dispatched from the Fatherland to head to the Indian Ocean and harass shipping up the east African coast. She had an amazing range of 12,750 nautical miles – about halfway around the world. That voyage would have been about 10,000 nautical miles and, at the time, the Germans were a bit light on filling stations east of Suez, so they probably counted on being refuelled by the Japanese or sticking up an Allied tanker.

Kapitänleutnant Heinz-Wilhelm Eck was ordered to proceed in utmost secrecy en route.

In the South Atlantic, they came across the Greek freighter SS *Pellus* and Eck just couldn't help himself. He waited until dark on 13 March 1944 and sent two torpedoes into the ship. She broke in half and was gone in three minutes. He took two surviving seamen aboard for interrogation and then tossed them back onto their raft.

Eck was concerned about the amount of floating debris which, he thought, would indicate his impulsive action and show signs of U-boat activity. He ordered the debris to be destroyed by grenades and gunfire.

It never seemed to enter his Teutonic mind that 35 crew members were clinging to the wreckage. Only three survived to be picked up after an astonishing 35 days adrift by a neutral Portuguese merchant ship and taken to Angola to tell their story.

On 1 April, just off South Africa, Eck came across the British merchant ship *Dahomian* with 5,000 tons of general war cargo and 17 precious aircraft. She was torpedoed and sunk ten miles off Cape Point. Two engineers were killed but the other 49 crew were saved by two South African Navy minesweepers.

There was a dramatic increase in air surveillance after the first U-boat attack in south and eastern African waters. Eck's radio signals were being picked up in Mombasa, Diego Garcia, Addu Atoll and the Seychelles. He managed to evade all the aerial searches until he was off the Somali Coast on 2 May, when he sent a long chatty message. His signals were picked up and six planes of 621 Squadron were scrambled.

A Wellington bomber from northern Somalia was experiencing low cloud and flew low and suddenly found a submarine surfacing in front of them. The radio operator notified all Allied bases from Aden to Mombasa and of course, when in pursuit of a sub, the Somali Camel Corps. He gave the position and the Wellington dived down to take on the U-boat head on. They raked the conning tower with gunfire and returned to drop two depth charges as the sub was diving.

Gotcha! There was an oil slick which would today earn an apoplectic outcry from environmentalists and U-852 began to resurface. It fired furiously at the Wellington and other aircraft that arrived from Aden to drop a total of 47 depth charges and unload 7,000 rounds of ammunition.

U-852 was sinking; to save the crew, Eck

"Come out and fight! We know you're in there..."

beached the sub but failed to blow her up just as the cavalry arrived. The Somali Camel Corps came lolloping over the sand dunes to capture the 59 crew. Eck destroyed the Enigma machine and codes, which was not as critical as it seemed at the time: Bletchley Park was looking over his shoulder at every keystroke. But he didn't destroy the logbook or his own diary which was a fatal mistake.

British Intelligence tied U-852 to the sinking of SS *Pellus* and the killing of survivors. Eck, the ship's doctor and Senior Officer Hoffman were executed for murder. Several other crewmen received terms from seven years to life. Eck claimed he was just tidying up the ocean from all that debris and was not following Admiral Doenitz's Laconia Order* which would actually have spared him the death penalty. This instructed U-boats not to pick up survivors of sunken ships. Really? After the Royal Navy picked him up having sunk his UN-68 in World War One? There's gratitude for you.

Even the Royal Navy failed to destroy the wreck of U-852 and sections of it can still be seen just south of Ras Hafun. I am sure when the Covid travel restrictions are over, tourists will be flocking back to Somalia and to those magnificent golden beaches I enjoyed years ago and will be able to check it out…

Tourists will be flocking back to those magnificent golden beaches

*MS *Laconia* was torpedoed off west Africa in 1942 by U-boats which stopped to rescue survivors and called for Allied shipping to help. US Captain Robert C Richardson III ordered aircraft to destroy the subs. 1,619 survivors died. I met one of the survivors on a ship as we crossed the exact location who gave a harrowing account of the events. The US declined to undertake any investigation.

HENRY V'S CHANNEL CRUISE

How early in advance do you plan your summer cruise?

11 August marks the anniversary of Henry V's departure to invade France and to reclaim lands he was convinced should be under English rule. Check Shakespeare for details – he pinched the facts from Hollingshead, a diligent and accurate historian. Henry V was flat broke and had seven ships in his Navy when he decided to go to war. All this was planned, executed and paid for within three months. Quirky is awed by the pre-planning and logistics. You might be too.

Henry goes into the bareboat charter business.
"OK, that's 2d a ton for three months, plus crew. Does the skipper's quarters come with an en suite?"

Don't you just love trivia quizzes?

I particularly enjoy the ones where the quiz master has pulled obscure facts from the internet that he did not know before, then lords it over the contestants as if he knew them all along and thinks he is the President of MENSA when we can't produce the answers up from our memory banks...

It is so much fun when they get it wrong. Like:

"No, the correct title of that painting is not *Whistler's Mother* but an *Arrangement in Grey And Black Number One*. And you have the apostrophe in the wrong place."

"Sorry Elton, 'Hakuna matata' does not mean 'No worries' in Swahili. A 'matata' is a civil uprising or riot. 'Worry' is 'wasiwasi'."

Then there is the Tie Breaker. When teams tying for first place have to guess an obscure number and whoever is closest wins. Our quiz master memorised the 1,665 steps up the Eiffel Tower and was so smug that we were 11 steps out. I felt compelled to act.

With an encouraging arm over his shoulder, I said: "You had some interesting questions earlier about Shakespeare's Henry V and the 100 Years' War. Yes, it was really 116, wasn't it? How many arrows did Henry take with him to Agincourt?"

"Er... 15,000...?"

"Slightly more. He took 8,982 archers with him. That's not quite two each."

"100,000?"

"Really? That would last the full army less than a minute. Even grounded with dysentery, the reduced English and Welsh archers fired a thousand arrows a second into the French."

Researchers, through the records of the day, reckon Henry packed between one and two *million* arrows in his luggage.

To supplement the ones that the English fletchers were churning out at six a day for three farthings each, Henry charged import duties not in cash, but in arrows and bow staves: ten Spanish or Italian yew staves for every ton of imports. Strangely, Mediterranean yew was preferred for making the English long bow.

England had prepared generations of bowmen by forbidding all sport except archery on Sundays. Any man who earnt more than two pounds a year was required to own a bow. If you could not fire ten arrows a minute and hit a target 100 yards away, you were considered a wimp and unfit for military service. The bow pull was 75 kilos. Get one of your gym-junky mates to demonstrate this: lift 75 kilos half a metre, twelve times a minute, with two fingers around a bit of string. The longbow could wound at 250 yards and kill at 100. Even through armour.

The arrow's metal barbs (or 'bodkins' against armour) were secured only with beeswax so the shaft could only be withdrawn

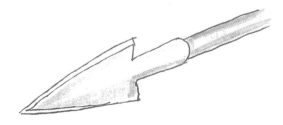

Traditional arrowhead

Bodkin for piercing armour – the square section head is wider than the shaft

To invade France, Dick Whittington helped Henry charter over 700 ships; guess what – most of them were French

without the head and the competition could not fire them back. They were shipped in circular leather collars of 24 to protect the flights. For a million arrows, that's over 40,000 batches.

Henry realised that his official Navy of seven ships would need a bit of help to get men and equipment across the Channel. He negotiated with the owners of merchant ships over 20 tons to charter their vessels at a rate of two shillings per ton per quarter. This was a bareboat charter; the crew was extra at 3d a day for seamen and 7d for masters. Some of the largest, stoutest ships were in the Bordeaux wine trade, many were French owned, but they still joined Henry's fleet. Even the faster defensive convoy protection vessels he used were French. That's like Churchill calling up Admiral Donitz just before D-Day and asking if he could borrow a couple of E-boats...

All he had to do now was to pay for it. He raised 130,000 pounds in 1415 money by hocking the family (crown) jewels and selling shares in the expedition which was basically a real estate and ransom venture. Among the investors in Henry V Inc. was the Lord Mayor of London, Dick Whittington. He was a very shrewd businessman and he and the City of London received a very good return. Yes, the same character in kids' stories and pantomimes really existed and actually became Mayor four times, not just the three in the story...

In his brilliant *Azincourt* Bernard Cornwell puts the invasion fleet at 1,500 but forensic accountants, digging through the records reckon there were 743 ships carrying 2,265 men at arms, 8,982 archers, the ships' crews of 2,566… and 18,000 horses (and no doubt a few jars of horseradish…), plus stores and weapons for all of the above.

That's food for 13,813 active blokes plus horse fodder. They crossed the Channel in just two days and made a more accurate landfall than we did 550 years later with a diesel engine, an ex-RAF compass and a School Cert in maths. These were fat, barrel-bilged ships, normally with a single square sail, loaded right down to their podgy gunwales and with the windward performance of a haystack. They arrived at Honfleur at the mouth of the Seine to find it barricaded by a boom of tree trunks. Henry was first ashore for legal reasons, advised by his lawyers. Something about him 'taking possession'. Cargos and contestants were discharged in three days. They reassembled their knocked-down IKEA-type wagons, loaded up and headed off to lay siege to Honfleur for five weeks… chewing up supplies, arrows and men.

Those who distrust French plumbing will not be surprised that Henry lost over a third of his troops to dysentery. He was now outnumbered 5:1 by the French and he offered to negotiate a surrender to spare his men the pain of battle. But they could not agree on the fine print, so he offered to settle the outcome with single-handed combat with the French King or Dauphin. Both wimped out. Henry was one tough cookie; at the Battle of Shrewsbury when he was sixteen, he copped an arrow through the cheek and fought on. He later endured the two weeks of agony it took to extract the arrowhead (see next chapter).

So on Friday, 25 October 1415, following some brilliant pre-battle planning, Henry did not quote Shakespeare. According to eyewitness accounts, the 28-year-old King just waved his sword and cried "C'mon lads, let's go."

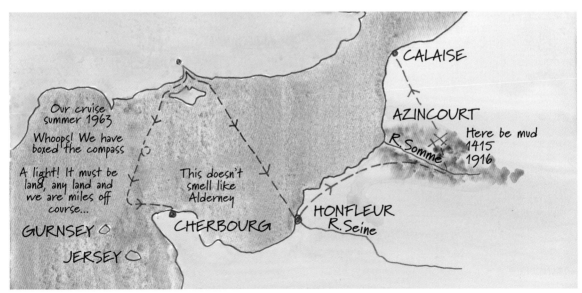

Henry V's Channel cruise compared with ours in 1963

THE TAMING OF THE SCREW

(You wouldn't believe how many titles we went through to get to this one: 'A brief history of...', 'One good...', etc.)

Following the mention of the successful removal of an arrowhead from Henry V's skull when the King's life depended on a threaded rod, Quirky was led into the history of this amazing invention and early precision metal working. Those of us who whinge about the cost of 316 stainless steel or bronze screws take note... we are lucky they are so cheap.

Henry V was an innovative ruler, not just because of the Kim Jong-un haircuts – he was the first English King to speak English; it was French up till then.

Henry V caught an arrow in the face at the Battle of Shrewsbury in 1403. The 16-year-old fought on with his team to win and the shaft was extracted after the battle, but the surgeons bodged their efforts to remove the arrowhead.

Today, 16 years old seems quite young to win a battle with an arrow sticking out of your face

He was trundled 65 miles (ouch!) to Kenilworth where Dr John Bradmore was summoned. He was renowned as a skilled surgeon and metal worker, often making his own tools for the job. His enthusiasm for metal working got him into trouble and he was sprung from jail for this op having been banged up for forging coins…

He spent two weeks widening the wound (ouch again…) to withdraw the arrowhead and made clever use of antiseptics of the day: rose honey and elder twigs in boiled linen. But no anaesthetics. He designed and made this special extraction tool using the Kenilworth Castle smithy. He forged the threads on the shaft. When this was cleaned up, he punched a hole in the thin metal of the tongs, heated them up and eased the threaded shaft through this metal frame, like a modern threaded tap, to create the thread.

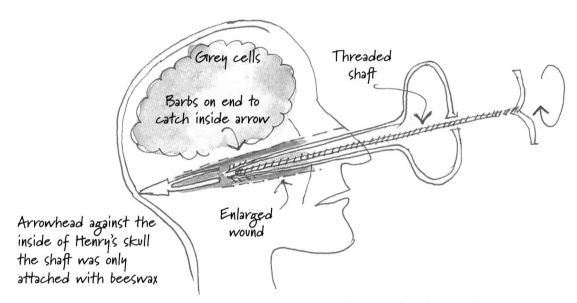

Dr Bradmore's home-made surgical instrument for Henry V's arrowhead extraction

Brilliant! Not many of us DIY boaties would be able to do this today even with a fistful of hardware store vouchers and today's modern tools and equipment.

Those of you who want to try this at home can see the video on Discovery Channel. If you can remember school Latin, read Bradmore's immaculately written instructions and sketches. His notes have just been found after 610 years. I have a similar filing system.

This was over 550 years before the National Health Service, so Bradmore was paid two pounds a year for life for this stunning op. (Interestingly, US Republicans berate the cost of the UK NHS as it devours 9.0% of GDP. How much does the US spend on public health care? 16.6% of GDP. But with their costs, you don't get much for your money.)

I had looked for answers on making early screw threads in a slim, modestly titled book *One Good Turn* which unfortunately goes straight from ancient history to the invention of screw-cutting lathes in the 1750s. The book's author has the very New York name of Witold Rybcznski and will be familiar to many of us. I am sure he is on my optician's Snellen chart too.

"I know this guy!"

The principle of the screw was known to the ancients. Archimedes was not able to take out a patent on the Archimedes Screw as it was in use well before he was born in 287 BC. It was reckoned to have provided the sprinkler system for the hanging gardens of Babylon as well as early bilge pumps. You would need boatbuilder's skills to make one of these as it relied on a waterproof spiral in a tube. They are very efficient and still used in Dutch drainage systems.

Timber screws were hand carved for wine and linen presses since Roman times. They cut the female block in half to chisel the threads then fastened the halves together, probably using trunnels (tree nails) with wedged ends. Try that in your evening school woodwork class.

Gunsmiths and clock makers made their own fine-threaded screws and coarser general-purpose ones were available, mainly for fixing locks and the newly invented butt hinge to doors. Blacksmiths produced forged steel screw blanks which were distributed to a domestic cottage industry where families cut a slot in the head with a hacksaw. Then the thread was filed by hand, often using a crude foot-powered spindle.

In 1760, two Midland brothers patented a screw-making machine where an automatic cutter could churn one out every seven seconds. In 1740 Britain produced less than a hundred gross screws annually. By Nelson's day, this was seven million gross.

Yet very few screws found their way into the shipyards. There were more screws in the officers' watches and navigation instruments than in the structure of HMS *Victory*. Boatbuilders preferred the security, cheapness and strength of clenched fastenings and trunnels. Only after the automotive industry used powered screwdrivers and square slotted screws in the twenties did US boatbuilders use screw fastenings for mass-produced light craft hulls.

The industrial revolution was fired by visionaries, often from humble backgrounds who dreamt up new machines, and then had to devise and make new tools to manufacture them.

Take the Yorkshire apprentice cloth maker Jesse Ramsden, who turned to making precision instruments. He spent 11 years building the first all-metal lathe to cut screw threads... and using the first diamond-tipped tools. His threads were accurate to one four-thousandth of an inch. In 1770, Ramsden made a sextant for another Yorkshire man, Captain James Cook. Its accuracy made it the leading GPS of its day.

How about the hefty blacksmith Henry Maudslay, son of a Kent wheelwright whose massive hands made a precision lathe to cut fifty threads an inch in a five-foot long two-inch rod. He built his own micrometre with a screw that could measure one ten thousandth of an inch.

He displayed examples of his work in his workshop window which caught the eye of a refugee immigrant. Frenchman Marc Isambard Brunel had escaped the French Revolutionary terror and was planning machines for mass producing ship's blocks for the Royal Navy in gratitude to the country that had taken him in.

With Maudslay's help, they built forty-four of them, some steam powered, with which ten unskilled men, instead of the previous 110 craftsmen, could manufacture the Navy's annual requirement of 160,000 blocks. Nelson was thrilled by this mechanisation when he inspected the production lines before he set off for the Battle of Trafalgar.

A sextant. "Jim, 'ere lad, tek this wi' you on your next trip. I'm working on my greatest invention yet: a machine to mek mushy peas."

"This thing I made is called a clock. I'm working on a smaller version that will fit in your pocket."
And he did – it only took him 46 years

Sorry Henry Ford, this odd couple was a century ahead of you.

This was quite a family team. As Marc Brunel's son, Isambard Kingdom, went on to devise inventions and machines that everyone needed for the Industrial Revolution, a sort of Victorian James Dyson, Maudslay's lads were there to build them. In 1838, they designed and built the engine for Brunel's *Great Western* steamship. At 750hp, it was the most powerful engine in the world.

Maudslay also made taxis until 1924 and I remember them still in service after the war.

For those of us who are in awe of the precision and skill of these early engineers and their metal working capabilities, be consoled that not all brilliant men were gifted in this medium. Remember John Harrison who made the first ship's chronometer and built his first accurate clock in 1713 at the age of 20?

It was made mostly of wood...

BOATS THAT FLY

War-winning aviation prompted by an art nouveau trophy

Quirky looks at the golden age of aviation when the fastest aircraft were water based. And amazingly, how a $2,000 prize and a rather florid trophy played their part in helping to save western democracy. He also gets back into doing the sort of drawings that filled his school exercise books.

It all started in 1912 when a French financier and seaplane enthusiast, Jacques Schneider, offered a prize of about $2,000 for technical advances made in civil aviation. It became an international speed race for water-based aircraft over a triangular course. The winner also received the Schneider Trophy, an exuberant example of the Art Nouveau period showing winged nymphs cosying up to Neptune. Have you seen this thing? What was second prize? Two weeks in Philadelphia? *

In 1917, a small but remarkable event occurred in the UK. On the swanky south coast, the head of what would become Supermarine Aviation Works, the socially aware and self-hyphenating Hubert Scott-Paine, hired a young engineer who later became the chief designer. The engineer was not university educated and had served an apprenticeship in a locomotive works. Worse, he qualified at night school. And he came from smoky Stoke-on-Trent in the

The Schneider Trophy.
"Can I swap it for an Amazon voucher?"

industrial Midlands with an accent to prove it. His name was Reg.

Reg was instructed to upgrade the Supermarine Baby flying boat which had won the 1922 event at 145.5mph for the forthcoming 1923 Schneider Trophy. The Baby had been built for the Navy who wanted a rugged spotter plane they could heave over the side and retrieve.

Flying boats can generally take rougher water conditions than float planes. They float on a boat-shaped fuselage rather than snap-off floats underneath. Part of the Schneider event called for sea trials in open water and many float planes broke up during these. However, the Baby, a pusher biplane with more rigging than *James Craig* (a square-rigged sail training ship)** was outclassed by Glenn Curtis's streamlined mono float

plane which won at 177mph. Four times the speed of the first event, just a decade ago. It also helped the Americans to overcome the embarrassment of not having a single combat aircraft in World War One.

The designer, Reg, Reginald James Mitchell, realised the built-in headwinds of a square-rigged biplane flying boat precluded it from future winners' stands. He guided Supermarine into sleek, stressed-skin monoplanes with minimal rigging on stepped floats... He made the fuselage so streamlined there was barely room for the pilot. Fuel had to be carried in the floats. He also worked with engine manufacturers to produce low profile engines of increasing power. Rolls Royce overtook Napier as the leading aero engine manufacturers with their intense devotion to the race.

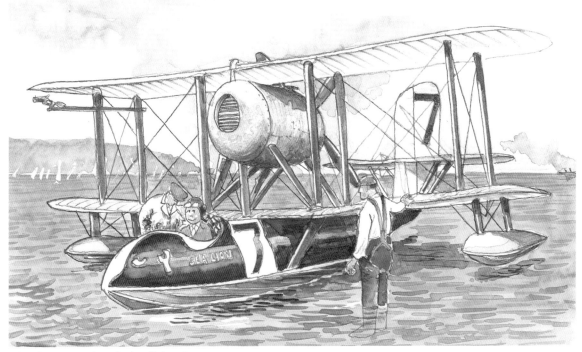

The Supermarine Baby flying boat.
"I love the kinky boots, Nigel."

Britain won the Cup in 1927 and 1929. If they won in 1931, they could keep it. Exciting, eh?

Imagine the Air Minister having a conversation with the equivalent of a Humphrey Appleby before the 1931 event.

AM: "I say, have you seen the aircraft Supermarine are planning for the Schneider Trophy we are hosting in the Solent? The S6B?"

HA: "Yes Minister."

AM: "An all-metal monoplane on floats with a 2,783hp 37-litre Rolls Royce V12 engine. I hear it's very fast and expected to beat the Americans, the Italians, the Germans and, thank God, the French."

HA: "Quite possibly, Minister."

AM: "Possibly? It does 380mph. Our front-line fighter is the Bristol Bulldog, a canvas covered biplane with a 440hp radial..."

HA: "Ah, but Minister, you are missing the point. The Bulldog was built to our express specification F20 / 27."

AM: "... but it is an open cockpit biplane that can only do 178mph..."

HA: "The open cockpit gives a chap a splendid view of the proceedings..."

AM: "But this S6B is so much more advanced, more powerful. It is over 100mph faster. And it's a seaplane; lugging a pair of boots the size of canal barges... This is really serious."

HA: "Indeed it is, Minister."

AM: "Does the Air Ministry have plans to deal with this?"

HA: "Of course, Minister. We have taken immediate steps. We have cut off all the public funding that the PM promised to Supermarine and Rolls Royce after their winning of the 1929 event. We have forbidden any member of the RAF High Speed Flight, which hitherto we have funded and have been specially trained for the event, from taking part. They will also not be allowed to use their 1929 winning aircraft. We have closed the Solent to the air race and will not be policing the event. So we can effectively consider the threat to be removed.

We simply cannot have private individuals such as aircraft companies and engine manufacturers building machines that are so superior to our specifications. It would make us look foolish. More importantly, it might give rise to some questioning the very role of the Air Ministry, Minister."

Lady Houston's generous funding came through only nine months before the 1931 Schneider Trophy race so there was no time to design a new aircraft. Mitchell refined the streamlining of the 1929 S6. The floats gave less drag by extending them and using them for part of the cooling system. The fuselage skin fitted the engine so smoothly that the pilot's view was between the two banks of cylinders. Rolls Royce squeezed an extra 400bhp from the massive 39.7 litre supercharged V12 on special aviation fuel... which it gargled at two gallons a minute. The improvements yielded a 49mph increase in speed to enable it to win... The S6B not only had to be aerodynamically smooth but also seaworthy and immensely strong. The landing speed was 95mph, so you must have been doing over a ton, heading into the wind on open water to take off. And the Solent can be pretty choppy, can't it? We once split a bottom plank heading into a wind against tide at 6 knots, so taking off at over 100mph... would be... exhilarating.

The S6B: You had to be doing at least 100mph for take off

Humphrey Appleby advancing Britain's aviation industry

prevailed. The Air Ministry folded, and half a million spectators flocked by public transport to watch the S6B win at 380mph on 13 September. A few days later it topped a world record breaking 400mph.

Still with floats.

The Schneider Trophy challenges brought another unexpected development which we will see in another chapter. The launches that attended and fussed around the British entry are reported to have had unreliable engines. One RAF fitter seemed to have a magic touch in keeping them going. He was a motorcycle enthusiast and, despite having a university education in archaeology, had a natural flair for engineering. (More about him in Chapter 10.)

Mitchell, together with Churchill and my dad, seemed to be the only people in the UK who were concerned about the threat of the ex-homeless failed art student ranting across

This may not have been the actual dialogue, but that was exactly what the Ministry did. Fortunately, the bountiful Lady Lucy Houston, an ex-East End chorus girl who startled her Jersey island neighbours by conspicuously working on her all over tan, kicked in a hundred thousand pounds out of the housekeeping. Lucy, eighth of ten children from a Lambeth slum, ran off to Paris at 16 with the heavily married heir to the Bass brewery. After that, she married well... And frequently.

An outraged press and public opinion

the Channel. Reg and his team set about using their experience in building the world's fastest aeroplane to building the world's best fighter. They didn't bother to meet the directives of any Air Ministry specifications. Just like Willie Messerschmitt, they only dealt with the challenges of aerodynamics, structural engineering and, over at Rolls Royce, thermodynamics. Their MD later said that two years' work on the Schneider challenge gave them the experience of six years of normal research.

Shut off from Government funding, Rolls financed private venture PV12, a 27-litre V12 super-charged engine to deliver a reliable 1,000hp. Following a line named after birds of prey, it would be called the Merlin. By brutally testing it to destruction, the Merlin earned a legendary name for power and reliability. The horsepower was eventually doubled, and squadrons of Lancaster bombers could fly to Berlin and back at full throttle.

In 1933, Mitchell underwent a major operation for cancer, but he returned to work to ensure the designs of Supermarine's Type 300 project were completed by December 1934 to allow construction of a prototype. At their own expense. One director noted this light powerful plane was likely to be a handful and difficult to control, "Just like my daughter. She's a real little spitfire..." Type 300 was renamed.

And the Air Ministry? They peered over Mitchell's shoulder and the following year issued their own cribbed specification F10 / 35 which seemed uncannily like one for the Supermarine project... They even provided some funds for the prototype... then, of course, they could then say it was 'built to their specifications'.

On 5 March 1936, the prototype took off for an eight-minute test flight. It achieved 349mph. Later that year, the Air Ministry issued the RAF with their new front-line fighters, built to their specs, of course: F7 /30... It was the quaint fabric covered biplane, the Gloster Gladiator. It could just stagger over 250mph. The Spitfire was heading for 400.

On 3 June 1937, a panicked Air Ministry ordered 310 Spitfires. Eight days later, Mitchell was dead at 42.

I may be more obliged to him, the Rolls Royce shareholders and M Schneider who started the whole development of racing seaplanes than most readers. I survived being born in a basement shelter during a raid by 441 bombers while our lads overhead fought for western democracy behind their Merlins with 80 gallons of 100 octane in their laps.

Fortunately, the bomb that landed outside the shelter was not a prime example of German engineering. It was as reliable as our German SUV, also a dud. That's one of the problems with slave labour, it's hard to maintain quality control and keep the workers enthused. I have since heard that wilful sabotage in the German slave factories was subtle and widespread. Very brave too. I mean, if you were found out, you wouldn't just lose your job, would you?

This bomb was on public display for many years, with a slot in it for collecting coins to rebuild a blitzed, battered and bankrupt Britain. The enemy, who had caused all this destruction, was awarded billions in Marshal Aid. So, eventually, was Britain. Today, many think that the American Lend Lease system, where a then neutral US passed weaponry to Britain who was standing alone against Hitler, was a gift. But it all had to be paid for. Often in gold. It took the UK until December 2006 to pay off the US Lend Lease war-time debt, plus interest.

Anyway, I think Reg, the ex-railway apprentice deserves a bit of a toast on 11 June, don't you?

---

*A comment by W C Fields when the first prize was one week in Philadelphia.
**James Craig, an iron square-rigged barque launched the year Churchill was born, restored and sailing in Sydney, Australia.

I'M SORRY, I HAVEN'T THE FOGGIEST

Just because your ship's bigger, doesn't mean your navigation is better

When caught out in fogs at sea, Quirky always errs on the side of total cowardice by slowing right down and listening for somebody else's engines. But some in the navy don't think you have to do that.

The sailing pilot cutters of the Bristol Channel were crafted by eye and built to put pilots aboard incoming ships at the entrance to the treacherous Bristol Channel. My respect for them increased vastly after our first wind against tide experience of the Channel in 1961. These engineless gaff cutters stayed at sea in all weathers and had to be fast enough to beat the competition and put their pilot on board arriving vessels before the opposition got there. So you can see that an immense amount of skill and seamanship was needed in these vessels.

Allowing for leeway under sail and the Channel tides running at up to eight knots, you can imagine their crews had a pretty good grasp of basic navigation.

"Looks clear enough, but just keep slow ahead..." (This happened to us in 1964)

The huge HMS Montagu *asked for the bearing to Hartland Point from the engineless cutter*

I have been an admirer of the supremely seaworthy Bristol Channel pilot cutters since school days. I built a sailing model of Dyarchy, for the grandchildren of course, which sits behind me as I write this.

One of these cutters was becalmed in fog at night on 29 May 1906 when they heard the approach of powerful engines. Out of the night emerged the vast bulk of the 15,000-ton battleship HMS *Montagu*. Fortunately, this pre-Dreadnought ship managed to stop before hitting the immobile and engineless cutter. The battleship had been anchored off Lundy Island on 27 May experimenting with receiving shore-based radio signals. None could be detected so she departed for the Scilly Isles. However, heavy fog was experienced, and she reversed course back to Lundy.

The cutter was hailed and asked for a bearing to Hartland Point, a popular graveyard of ships on the North Devon coast.

This was accurately given but the information was scoffed at by the navigating officer because it did not match his dead reckoning position. Have a look at the map. He was probably belting along on a north-easterly reciprocal course, about three miles from Lundy when the dumb idiots in the cutter told them Hartland Point was south-southeast of where they were. He was aboard one of the mightiest and fastest warships afloat, 432 feet of armour-plated steel, with lots of guns and a radio. It had engines, electricity, hot and cold running water and everything. The cutter was a quaint, engineless vegetable fibre relic, lit by whale oil and using Elizabethan technology.

The Navy ship ignored the advice and resumed her original course despite one of the Westernmen, as they called Bristol

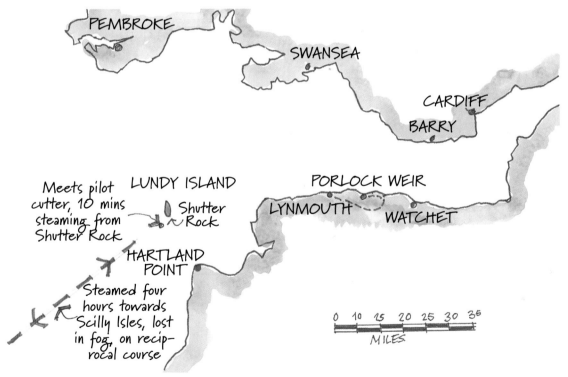

HMS Montagu's *course that night and the overland route of the Lynmouth lifeboat in the next chapter*

Channel pilots, warning "You'm carry on on that course and you'm gunner be on Shutter Rocks in ten minutes."

It was slightly less than that when the Westernmen heard the unmistakable sound of an expensive battleship trying to mount an immovable rock.

She hit so hard and so fast that she ripped a 91-foot hole in her armoured hull and stove it in ten feet. HMS *Montagu* had cost the British taxpayers 1,046,992 quid just five years before. That was real money in those days, but from what I hear, this barely covers the cost of an annual commuter season ticket now.

The impact toppled the topmast to which her fine new aerial was attached and put the radio out of action. The captain was convinced he had hit Hartland Point which is guarded by a lighthouse on its northern side. He ordered a rowing boat to be launched and commanded the crew to pull to the lighthouse and instruct the keeper to send a wireless message to the Admiralty saying that *Montagu* was in a spot of bother on Hartland Point.

They found the lighthouse where they expected it, but the keeper was another one of those dumb West Country bumpkins. A heated argument developed when he insisted that he was not the keeper of the Hartland Point Lighthouse. They keep that over on Hartland Point, 11 miles away. He was definitely the keeper of the Lundy Island Light which, as far as he could remember, has always been on Lundy. He had just heard them run aground on Shutter Rock. This is also on Lundy. Right at the southern end.

If you think that was a stuffed-up debacle, it was nothing compared with the salvage attempts. The Navy did not have its own salvage arm and thought that this would be a great excuse to start one.

Their Lordships consulted the best textbook on the subject written by Frederick Young, Britain's top salvage expert who worked with The Liverpool Salvage Company.

They made him a Commodore and put him in charge… but under an Admiral who had no experience in salvage but insisted on using his own ideas. Rather like internet scientists today who can find more cures for Covid in a few minutes online than the most experienced medics and universities have ever heard about.

The Admiral was surprised that his idea of filling the hull with cork did not lift the 15,000-ton waterlogged deadweight. But it did a great job of clogging the pumps. While they were faffing around adamantly refusing Young's experienced advice, the ship began to break up and became a total loss. A Cornish salvage firm was called in to dismantle and clean up the wreck.

It took them 15 years.

But is not just the Royal Navy that can stuff up their navigation and run expensive ships into total destruction, the US can do it too. But being Americans, theirs had to be a bigger, better, faster and more expensive stuff-up.

On 8 September 1923, 14 destroyers, just five years old and of the 35-knot Clemson class were steaming south from San Francisco to San Diego. Some of this type were later transferred to the UK in World War Two as part of the Lend Lease arrangement. They were fast for their day and had a long 4,900-mile range but this came with saving weight by having limited armour and locating vulnerable long range fuel tanks in the sides above the waterline.

At 9:00pm they turned east, aiming for the Santa Barbara Channel. USS *Delphy* had a radio navigation receiver but her captain, Lieutenant Commander Donald T Hunter, who was acting as the squadron's navigator,

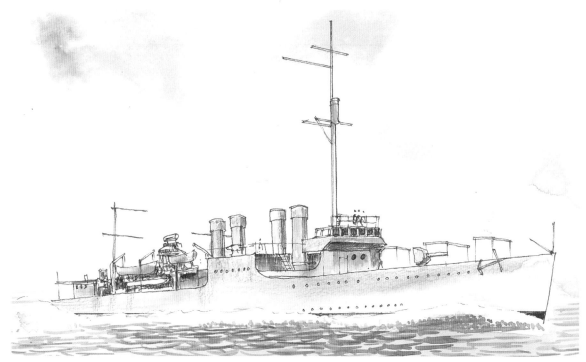

The Clemson class destroyers achieved 35 knots and a range of 4,900 miles from light weight, little armour and large fuel tanks above the water

distrusted this new-fangled device and believed the readings to be in error. After all, they did not agree with his dead reckoning which he carefully calculated by measuring the rpm of the propellers.

Really? That may give you the speed through the water, but aren't there are a few other considerations to take into account? Windage, leeway, tides and currents?

The ships were on an exercise to simulate war-time conditions. Even in the strong winds and heavy seas that night, visibility was suddenly decreased by heavy fog rolling in, as it does on that section of the California coast. They continued at speed – there was a pretend war on. They didn't bother to take soundings with their electronic fathometer because they would have had to slow down to do that.

Sea conditions and seamanship are impervious to political situations. Common sense requires that the same standards of care are maintained whether its war time or Christmas. I worked in east Asia when ferries, for a certain er… financial consideration, are granted permission to carry far more than their legal number of passengers at holiday times. Then we see the tragic results on the World News.

So it's into the Santa Barbara Channel at night and in fog, 14 destroyers in close formation at 20 knots. However, the lead ship, *Delphy*, had turned a bit too soon and ran hard aground. Above the sound of scraping hulls and spilt coffee cups there was a vigorous sounding of sirens which allowed some of the ships at the tail of the convoy to avoid grounding.

The last five ships were commanded by

Commander Walter Roper in USS *Kennedy*. He believed the accurate fixes shown by the radio bearings and ordered them to slow down and then to stop to avoid running onto the rocks. Seven of the lead ships ran aground and were totally wrecked with a loss of life of 23 sailors. Two of the others limped off the rocks with minor damage. That's seven ships lost in one go. A peacetime best for the US Navy.

They had just missed the Santa Barbara Channel by a bit. They were on the rocks at Honda Point, also known as Pedenales Point, a mere 56 miles to the north of the Channel in a sea passage of 350 miles. Many of the crews were saved by brave and innovative local ranchers who rigged breeches buoys from the cliffs to haul them to safety. The ships that didn't ground picked up survivors who had been thrown into the sea.

As well as the greatest peace-time loss, 11 was also the largest number of officers on trial at one court martial. Captain Watson was in charge of the flotilla, had his flag in *Delphy* and was accountable for all navigational decisions. He took full responsibility for ordering the change of course. He was stripped of seniority and three of the other officers were admonished. Commander Roper was given a letter of commendation for his navigational skill which would no doubt encourage other navigators to trust in the accuracy of the modern equipment.

The steamer SS *Cuba* had grounded nearby on the same day, and many blamed the Tokyo earthquake that had occurred the previous week for creating abnormal currents along the California coast. Nobody seemed to raise the danger of 14 ships proceeding at high speed in poor visibility at night in an area thick with coastal shipping. Many vessels, particularly in the timber trade, were wooden sailing ships and would have been unable to avoid any on-coming dangers.

So even if you have the latest up-to-date whiz-bang radar, just ease the throttle when the visibility thickens. Just in case somebody's little wooden dinghy does not show up on it.

It might be mine.

My little wooden dinghy following Pete Culler's design for the longboats for a replica of the schooner America. *I lofted and built the hull in 59½ hours. It took just two and a half years to finish it!*

THE GREAT LYNMOUTH LIFEBOAT RESCUE

I'm glad I don't need to go to so much trouble to launch my boat

12 January marks the anniversary of one of the greatest lifeboat feats ever recorded. Quirky looks into some unexplained aspects of this and traces its antipodean aftermath. The rescue involved two of his favourite harbours in the Bristol Channel.

After 12 hours, the lifeboat was finally launched

It was a dark and stormy night… (I use this opening purely because we were strictly told at school never to begin with this line as it is a corny cliché. However, Alexander Dumas started Chapter 65 of *The Three Musketeers* with this, and nobody gave him a detention for it.) Anyway, those were the meteorological conditions prevailing at the time, at 6:30pm on Thursday, 12 January 1899. The notorious Bristol Channel with its vicious tides copped the full impact of storm force winds (Force 10 = 55 knots and above) and impenetrable rain. It destroyed the brand-new steamer pier at Woody Bay, two miles from Lynmouth. The stumps are still visible at low tide.

Forrest Hall was a substantial, three-masted, full-rigged iron ship of 2,052 gross registered tons (*James Craig*, Chapter 4, is about 670) being towed from Bristol to Liverpool for repairs when she lost her rudder and the tow line parted. She dropped anchors and began dragging onto a lee shore in Porlock Bay towards Hurlstone Point. A telegram was received at Lynmouth at 7:52pm saying that the Watchet lifeboat was unable to launch due to the storm, could Lynmouth help?

Why didn't the tug, with presumably enough coal to reach Liverpool, try to get another line aboard? And what did it do for the next 18 hours? Why send for a 34-foot wooden rowing boat when the steam tug was presumably close by?

The Lynmouth coxswain, Jack Crowcombe, realised it would be impossible to attempt to launch *Louisa*, the 34-foot double-ended lifeboat in these conditions. He suggested the only way to reach the stricken vessel would be to haul her on her carriage, overland and attempt to launch her at Porlock which was slightly protected from the westerly storm. This is a distance of 13 miles involving what is

still the steepest A road in England. A gentler sloped toll road was available with only a 1-in-17 gradient but a mile extra in length. History does not record why this easier route was not used. Did nobody have correct change for the toll? Also, Watchet was a similar distance from the ship and via a reasonably level road. Astonishingly, the boat challenged by some of the steepest and most twisting lanes in England was the one that responded.

Word was passed up to the larger village of Lynton, perched above Lynmouth Harbour, appealing for help and horses. About 100 volunteers and 18 horses set off to haul the ten-ton boat and carriage up Countisbury Hill. Six men with shovels went ahead to widen the road.

The convoy reached the Blue Ball Inn, around 1,423 feet or 340m above sea level where a broken wheel was repaired. The pub is still open today but would probably struggle to cope with the thirsts and appetites of 100 exhausted walk-ins at 2:00am. Nevertheless, the whole group was refreshed. In fact, most thought that they had done the hard part, it would be on the level or all downhill after this. So they staggered off home including the women and children, leaving 20 men to handle the boat and carriage, along with the lifeboat crew of 15.

This was only a mile and a half from Lynmouth! Yes, it was pretty level across the top of Exmoor, but it was another 11 miles including Porlock Hill, the steepest, twistiest hill in England. The lifeboat was transferred to skids at the top to prevent her running away. An owner consented to the corner of his cottage to be hacked away. A number of stone walls were demolished.

At the bottom of the notorious 1-in-4 hill, it was still two miles to the harbour at Porlock Weir, a chocolate-box beauty of a harbour.

"So that's 114 pints, 300 packets of chips, 200 pies, a dry sherry for the vicar... and who is the Diet Coke?"

The access to this dries out below half tide. So *Louisa* was heaved onto the very rocky Porlock Beach and launched directly into the surf. This was after nearly 12 hours of hauling her over one of the most difficult roads in Britain in the worst storm since the killer one of 1891.

It took them an hour to row out to the ship and they stood by all day, using their oars to stay alongside her until two steam tugs arrived and secured new tow lines.

The ship's crew said they were too exhausted to raise the anchor so some of the lifeboat men, who had been hauling and rowing their boat for 15 hours, climbed aboard the heaving ship to help. It took until 5:00pm to reach Barry across the Channel. A steamer then towed *Louisa* and her exhausted crew back to Lynmouth where they arrived 41 hours after leaving.

A century earlier, England had coined an expression about their Navy, saying they were protected by wooden walls and iron men. I reckon the whole population of Lynmouth and Lynton who took part qualify as iron men. Particularly the women and children. However, those who ran the Royal National Lifeboat Institute didn't think the volunteer crew qualified for any official recognition. They had been awarding gold medals since 1834 but none were handed out over the amazing feat which still sends tingles through me as I write about it. It happened just over 40 years before I was born, and I remember the old Lynmouth lifeboat in its shed with the slipway reaching down to the low-tide mark before it was demolished at the end of 1944.

R H Fry, the owner of *Forrest Hall*, dished out gold watches and chains to the coxswain and second cox, silver ones to the rest of the crew plus five pounds each, probably a month's money for these West Country folk. He shelled out twenty-seven pounds five shillings and sixpence to repair all the damage to walls and buildings. Sadly, four horses died during the event. I can find no record of compensation for them.

It seems that *Forrest Hall* ran aground more often than me. She survived a range of groundings from Calcutta to Bristol but met her fate in New Zealand ten years later. Her skipper managed to put her aground on a weather shore in light winds and perfect visibility. In February 1909, she was delivering 3,127 tons of Hunter Valley's finest (coal, not wine) from Newcastle to Chile by way of the northern tip of North Island. 15 miles from 90 Mile Beach the First Officer suggested to Captain John Fenn Collins that the ship be tacked. The captain refused and kept on course. When 4½ miles off the shore, the First Officer made the decision to put the ship about. Amazingly, the skipper overruled this and went back to the original course. Under full sail, it only took three minutes to ground on the weather shore of 90 Mile Beach. The crew was saved and looked after so well by Maori villagers that they were awarded the ship's bell. It is still used at TeHapeu School in Parengarrenga. As an extra bonus the ship generously discharged her cargo of coal during storms over the years onto the beach to the grateful residents.

Forrest Hall's *final demise in New Zealand*

Amazingly, the skipper only lost his ticket for two years, but it's not the thing you would want on your CV is it? He also had to pay the costs of the enquiry. The most damning evidence came from the Third Officer, Charles Collins, who stated that the captain was a drunk and prone to epileptic fits. He should know. He was his brother.

I have happy memories of cruising between Porlock Weir and Lynmouth. The current owners of my Dad's 1938 motor cruiser *Ryegate* also have a 1938 SS Jaguar. I am trying to arrange a photoshoot of the two of them without using Photoshop.

For now I have to use my imagination

THE MAN WHO 'HID' THE SUEZ CANAL (OR SO HE SAID)

Mis-information (fake news) has always been part of fighting a war

The office manageress of the architectural office where I worked in Nairobi was delightful and efficient. But she wasn't always the staid fifty-something matron. After a couple of pre-Christmas sherries, she let slip that in her youth she was a showgirl who was sawn in half twice nightly, by Jasper Maskelyne in spangled tights. (Her, not him.) Quirky checks some of Jasper's claimed war-time achievements and wanders off into a few family reminiscences.

Jasper Maskelyne's peace-time party trick: he sawed our office manageress in half, twice nightly

It sounds like a Tommy Cooper line, but when Jasper Maskelyne, the noted third generation London magician, volunteered for military service aged 37 in 1940, he was sent to the camouflage school in Farnham Castle... "But I couldn't find it ..."

Actually, he did. He claimed he so impressed a visiting Lord Gort by hiding a machine gun nest in an open meadow, Jasper next found himself seconded to MI9 (escape and evasion) in meadow-less Egypt.

So I set about researching this and found that the Australian film director Peter Weir planned to make a film about it with Benedict Cumberbatch... Wow! How exciting...

But it was abandoned.

Why?

Unfortunately, Jasper's war-time recollections do not stack up with the official versions. Even his son, a retired airline pilot in Queensland, acknowledged that his father's book *Magic: Top Secret* was mainly the imagination of his ghost writer. It was written for the express purpose of being a bestseller to get Maskelyne out of a financial hole with the British tax authorities. By a remarkable series of events, the editor of *Old Africa Magazine*, to which I contribute, has a copy of this rare book which actually belonged to Jasper's widow.

According to the book, Maskelyne claimed that on arrival in Egypt, he was asked to hide vital war-time material from the Germans.

'How about Alexandria Harbour?', he writes. Allied supply ships all discharged at this main port, and it was a natural target.

So he claims the 'Magic Gang' was formed. Just like in the *Goon Show* episode 'Tales of Old Dartmoor', they built a cardboard (canvas actually) replica of Alexandria, at Marint Bay, a brackish lake quite close to the harbour. It was supposedly wired for Son et Lumière by being lit up like the real thing, while Alexandria itself was under total blackout. When the first German bombers droned overhead on a night raid, they saw the lights of the harbour under what they thought was sloppy blackout discipline. Then they also saw explosions which were Jasper's pyrotechnics.

"Gott im Himmel. Our leader has hit a fuel dump!" The air crews thought that others had started bombing the target and they unloaded everything they had. They did this while vital supplies were safely unloaded in Alexandria.

So you can see why Peter Weir wanted to make a film of this, can't you?

The most vulnerable and valuable asset in the Empire then was the Suez Canal. Without that, Britain's lifeline with the Commonwealth was severed.

"Can't move it", claimed Maskelyne. "But we can try to hide it. I think we can modify that lighting trick that granddad created in 1885 to use strobe lights to baffle the audience."

He says he borrowed 21 searchlights and set them up along the canal. They were equipped with a series of rotating reflectors to provide a primitive strobe effect. When Maskelyne tested this in a night flight, it was reported that the pilot became disoriented by them and almost lost control of the aircraft before levelling out just above the desert.

Sorry Jasper, can't find any record of this and using that number of searchlights although, amazingly, the hundred odd mile stretch of canal remained unharmed throughout the war.

But there is one claim that is dismissed by many as never having happened: they poo-pooed the idea that Maskelyne ordered tons of explosive camel poo which was scattered around Rommel's camp and accounted for numerous casualties among his vehicles and damaged troop morale.

This criticism is of particular interest to me. My late father-in-law, Charles Fraser-Smith (CFS), designed and supplied the explosive droppings. Tons and tons of them.

He had arrived in the UK from Morocco in 1941 when France fell, where he had been, among other things, Keeper of The King's Estates. He was fluent in French and Arabic. And, as a farmer, he knew all about animal droppings. He escaped aboard a Norwegian fertiliser ship in a convoy that was bombed… by our allies, the French. They were a bit upset about Churchill's demands that the French Mediterranean Fleet should sail to neutral ports to avoid falling into German hands. In a fit of Gallic pride, they refused.

Explosive animal droppings produced by the bucket-load

In a fit of pragmatic necessity, Churchill ordered the Royal Navy to sink the fleet at Mers-el-Kebir. This unfortunately cost the lives of 1,200 French sailors...

While lecturing to a bored bunch of Avro employees on metric conversion, CFS was approached by two homburgs and overcoats who asked him if he would like to do something more interesting. Just sign this Official Secrets Act they said, it will only last until 30 years after the war and whisked him off to London.

There he was asked how many devices he could get into a fountain pen that might be of use to agents behind the lines. He designed and made gadgets for all arms of the services. Even for the creator of James Bond 007, Ian Fleming.

CFS produced the canister in which The Man Who Never Was went to war, packed in dry ice. He and his neighbour, Sir Bernard Spilsbury, the Home Office pathologist, strolled to the same railway station every morning, not knowing they were both working on the same secret project. Spilsbury was involved with sourcing a convincing body. Sadly, when he became too ill to work, he inhaled his Bunsen burner in 1947 and CFS did not know about the success of Operation Mincemeat until well after the war.

The explosive animal droppings were used not only in north Africa but also in France to slow down German reinforcements reaching the D-Day beaches. It was easier to

Tanks disguised as trucks...

... and inflatable tanks

sprinkle these on a road than to try to bury landmines. Some had convincing tyre tracks through them to look aged.

CFS said German practice runs could get reinforcements from the south of France to Normandy in three days. After the landings, one convoy took 17 days... and lost most of their vehicles en route. All the records of British Military Exploding Animal Droppings were probably contained solely within his coded black notebook which the family have loaned out for a number of military exhibitions.

When French engine drivers were all replaced by Germans, he produced explosive coal. This was scattered into railway yards by French children and later gave satisfyingly spectacular pyrotechnic results.

Maskelyne's greatest triumph was claimed to be worked out with Monty. The Magic Gang, now joined by scenery experts from British film studios, built prefab covers for 600 tanks to make them look like trucks. They could be driven, dressed up like a truck, and yet leave perfect tyre tracks. And the trucks disguised as tanks left tank tracks. All this is true.

Did it work?

Check out the score of the Battle of Alamein and how this deception really outfoxed The Desert Fox.

People involved in secret military stuff, like CFS don't get accolades after the event, although after the publication of his book, *The Secret War of Charles Fraser-Smith*, he became a minor celebrity. He was interviewed

Q (Desmond Llewellyn) and my late father-in-law, Charles Fraser-Smith

by *60 Minutes* from the US on how he made a duplicate uniform for Rudolph Hesse and then featured in a BBC TV programme where he and Desmond Llewellyn (Q in the James Bond films) compared escape and evasion devices from World War Two and the Bond films. (Llewellyn said he wished he had met CFS earlier, as he spent the last years of the war in a German POW camp.)

Maskelyne claims he got more recognition from the enemy than he did from the army when he alleged Hitler ordered his assassination. However, for his post-war stage performances, Jasper was apparently officially allowed to appear in full military dress uniform. One cynical *Guardian* critic said that he resented his lack of acclaim: 'For a vain man, this lack of recognition was intolerable and he died an embittered drunk in Kenya.'

Not according to our office manager. He loved life and performing, right up to the end. Well, and a drink or two...

But if your aim was to be a drunk in those post-war days, I can think of no finer place in which to practise your art.

Jasper and the company set off for a safari to Cape Town and back. Note the fashions of the day: Ladies with gloves and suits (called 'costumes' then), blokes with cravats and wide-open neck shirts that looked like you had a dead seagull on your shoulder. Not very Stewart Granger-ish, is it?

WARNING SHOTS

Why a Christmas tree ends up in Trafalgar Square each Christmas

Remember that line in the musical Chicago *when the woman prisoner said she fired a warning shot... "Right into his head"? Look for the Norwegian film* The King's Choice *and you will see how two antiquated shells and an obsolete torpedo made their mark on history.*

We are a classy lot on the creek at Patonga. Just because you don't see us wearing ties or matching socks doesn't mean we haven't got it by the bucket load. Our neighbour, for example, just casually mentioned that his grandfather had been knighted by King Haakon VII of Norway. A European knighthood? How classy is that? So when the story of Haakon's escape from the German invasion in the film *The King's Choice* was released, we just had to see it.

Germany trampled their jack boots over this strictly neutral country in 1940 'to save it', they said, 'from a British invasion.' They sneaked a flotilla of warships up the Oslofjord at night lead by *Blücher*, a heavy cruiser that had only been commissioned to be ready for sea three days before. She still had shipyard workers on board doing finishing touches.

As *Blücher* (yes, quite right, you at the back there, she was named after the Prussian who arrived in the nick of time at

So how long have you been in the Army, lad? Any experience in artillary?

Since Wednesday sir. Not really. Catering Corps

But I can make a really mean Bombe Alaska...

Oslo was defended by weapons bought at a closing down sale of the Austro-Hungarian Empire; and manned by new recruits from the catering corps

Waterloo) passed the first defensive battery, her identity was unknown so, following the rules of the Geneva Convention, warning shots were fired. *Blücher* ignored them and steamed on. The word was passed to other shore batteries.

When she came within 1,800 metres of the Oscarsbourg battery, the 64-year-old Colonel Birger Erikson faced a problem. His battery was a hundred years old and fitted with old second-hand 11" guns whose warranty had expired with the Austro-Hungarian Empire, from whom they were bought in a closing down sale. The shells were also bargain-basement specials from the old Empire. The only new supplies were the 30 young soldiers that he roused out of bed on that freezing morning of 9 April. Apart from one artillery officer, they had joined the army seven days before, had no gunnery experience and could not reload the guns. They were in the catering corps.

The only shells he could fire were those up the spout. If he fired warning shots, he would have nothing left. Dammit, he thought to himself in Norwegian, 'That ship, whatever nationality she is, just sailed past warning shots from the other battery.'

"I will either be decorated, or court martialled... Fire!"

His first warning shot plunged into *Blücher's* hull just forward of the aft mast and exploded in the magazine. This also happened to contain oil, smoke dispensers, incendiary bombs, aircraft bombs, depth charges, aviation fuel and two Arado seaplanes.

The second one blew the forward turret overboard and knocked out all the ship's electrics which powered the heavy guns. They could not be fired.

All textbook stuff.

Blücher was now ablaze and out of the battery gunnery range but only 500 metres away from another one armed with possibly the oldest and most travelled torpedoes in the world. Made in the 1890s they also came from an Austro-Hungarian garage sale and had been test fired over 200 times in training sessions.

Now fitted with live warheads, they were probably equally dangerous at either end. The officer in charge was away sick, so an old pensioner was roused who had been retired from the Navy since 1928. He started on torpedoes in 1909 and knew about these Austrian antiques. He aimed by eye and experience and fired them both. They hit below where the shells had struck, blew out any remaining bulkheads and stopped the engines.

Blücher then fired all her torpedoes. Not at anything in particular, just to get rid of the damned things so they didn't blow up from the fires that were now raging from end to end. Within minutes, she turned over and sank.

The following flotilla, seeing this impressive firework display, thought the fjord was packed with mines, turned and fled, which briefly postponed the invasion.

A country with the population of Scunthorpe United's supporters' club had destroyed the Kriegsmarine's brand new 17,820-ton, 32-knot heavy cruiser. Blown to bits, while the paint was still wet, with armaments from the Austro-Hungarian reject shop, manned by a couple of pensioners and raw recruits, many of whom were pulled from the kitchens to man the guns.

Blücher suffered nearly a thousand casualties, including most of the Gestapo and Nazi officials who were jammed in on their way to bring the same enlightened government to Oslo as they had to the rest of Europe.

This delay gave vital hours for the King and his government to escape, unlike his family who were allowed temporary asylum in Sweden: his daughter-in-law was a Swedish Princess. Sweden was supposedly neutral, however, the Princess thought they were neutral but on the German side. She and her children accepted an invitation to stay with friends she had met on a US tour. Her hosts had plenty of room in their big white house at 1,600 Pennsylvania Avenue and the huge collection of ship models fascinated three-year-old Prince Harald, a lifelong sailor. After all, Franklin Delano Roosevelt (FDR) had been Secretary of the Navy for 13 years. Check out the *Atlantic Crossing* series on your TV.

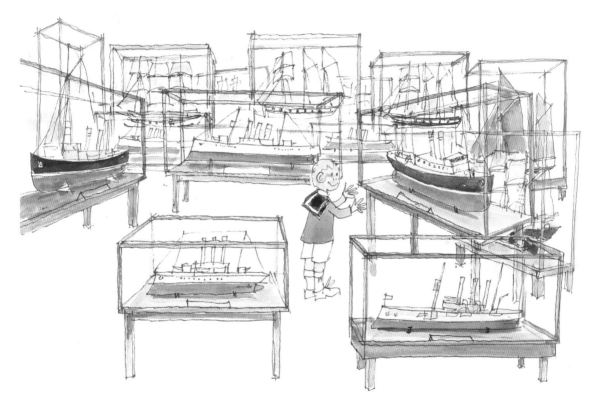

Three-year-old Prince Harald was fascinated by the ship models in the White House

The King and his cabinet were on the run for an astonishing two months, being hidden and supplied by loyal subjects. They camouflaged their getaway cars by daubing them white, hid in tunnels from countless dive bomber attacks and escaped while being chased by over 100 paratrooper hit men that Hitler sent after them. Haakon refused German demands to be a puppet ruler in a Nazi regime under Vidkun Quisling, who headed a domestic Nazi collaborationist regime during World War Two. The name has entered the dictionary as a noun and an adjective of derision.

The King on the run (this actually happened)

The King and Co were eventually rescued by HMS *Devonshire* from Tromsø, 200 miles north of the Arctic Circle sent by the King's nephew, George VI, and brought to Britain. Not only the King and his government ministers but also three naval ships with 500 crew and five aircraft escaped to join the Allies. But this came at a horrific cost. The nearby heavy carrier HMS *Glorious* and two destroyers, *Ascata* and *Ardent*, were sunk with the loss of 1,519 sailors. Of the 900 who survived the sinking of *Glorious* and the others, only about 40 were rescued, not by the Germans (who did not pick up survivors) but by the Norwegian ship *Borgund* and brave local fishing boats.

The elusive and convoy-killing German battleship *Scharnhorst* was later sunk by a posse of Royal Navy ships staging a dangerous, but very successful, trap off North Cape, the frozen tip of Norway on Boxing Day 1943. Allied destroyers who finished her off included HNoMS *Stord*, a gift to the Norwegians by Britain. They rescued 36 out of the 1,968 crew. We were there on Midsummer Day, and it was barely above freezing. Firstly, I am surprised that they bothered to rescue the Germans after what they did, and you would have thought they would have been snap frozen after a few minutes in that water.

After the King's escape, a furious Quisling instructed the skipper of every Norwegian ship not in home waters report to a German-controlled port.

Guess how many did?

Not one.

Oh, and in 1945 Quisling's severance package from the Norwegian people included a free firing squad.

The King was followed by every single Norwegian merchant ship that could evade the Germans. From exile in London, this tiny nation set up the world's largest merchant fleet for use by the Allies. The mighty US had 1,340 merchant ships at the time; Norway had a thousand, manned by 30,000 sailors each one with a grudge against the Nazis.

They fuelled the Battle of Britain.

They helped to bring countless tons of US fuel for the Royal Navy, high octane aviation fuel and another million tons a week of essential supplies… With every Spitfire's Merlin engine gargling its way through a gallon of 100 octane a minute, you can't just pop down to your local fuel station with a couple of cans to fill her up.

80 gallons of 100 please...

You can't just pop down to your local petrol station to refuel your Spitfire

Those accurate warning shots in Norway that turned round the invasion flotilla and saved the King can be seen as a vital change in the history of the war for Britain. The Norwegian Fleet was vital in the Battle of the Atlantic.

Every year since 1947, the people of Oslo send the people of Britain a present: a 20m Norwegian spruce Christmas tree which is displayed in Trafalgar Square. The accompanying card reads, 'Thanks for your support 1940-45'. This prime handpicked tree is the gold standard of timber for making spars and masts. A British boating magazine proposed a plan by which the tree is given to spar makers in exchange for sponsoring apprenticeships for boatbuilders and shipwrights. Unfortunately, the Mayor of London's office showed no interest. This magnificent timber is wood chipped for mulch like junked packing cases.

You will be able to find the film on one of your specialised TV channels, but when you see it, wrap up well. After watching 2 hours and 20 minutes of snow and ice, my wife and I were so involved we nearly went down with hypothermia.

THE BIRTH OF THE US NAVY

The US Navy was started for a very American reason: to take down a protection racket

I was recently laid up on a US ship and their library offered an interesting history about the start of their Navy. Did you know that the term 'US' only came into general use after Gettysburg in 1863? Up till then it was always 'America'.

After the War of Independence from Britain in 1783 America was so broke, it sold off its Navy. Their frigate *Alliance* fetched $26,000 at auction in 1785, but like any nation in this situation, they needed export markets to bring in some cash. US shipping had been protected by Britain until then.

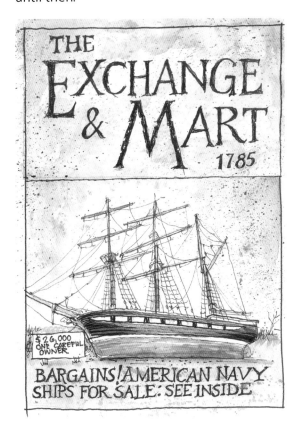

In 1785 the US sold off its Navy

So when Barbary Coast ships seized three American merchantmen in 1784 and imprisoned their crews, President Jefferson sent envoys to negotiate their release. The Barbary States demanded $600,000 protection money. That was serious money then – one sixth of the US budget at the time when the population was 5.3 million. Through skilful negotiations by the civil service of the day, they tried to palm them off with $40,000. Negotiations dragged on for a decade while the captives languished as slaves and the payment had been upped to over a million dollars.

In 1786, Jefferson and John Adams met Tripoli's envoy in London. (By the way, did you realise that both these gents died on the same day? Patriotically, it was 4 June 1836, exactly 50 years after signing the Declaration of Independence. Keep reading this book – you will always learn something useless!) They asked, "Why do the Barbary States make war upon nations who had done them no injury?"

"It is in our Holy Book. Any nations that do not acknowledge the Prophet are sinners and it is our rightful duty to plunder and enslave them."

"So it's for religious reasons?"

"Yes, plus I get a commission on the protection money."

Seriously! He bragged to them what his cut would be.

It took 15 years for Congress to do the sums and work out that for the price of paying annual protection, they could have their own Navy. In 1794, they allocated a miserly precise $688,888.82 to build four 44-gun frigates and two 36-gun ones. Unless, of course, satisfactory terms could be agreed with the Barbary States.

Congress agreed to the spending on the six ships, they were built in six different locations to spread the funding around and they were built to a very high standard. This specified white pine, longleaf yellow pine (known as pitch pine in the UK), white oak and southern live oak for the framing. This is an evergreen oak and extremely dense and strong. It is 50% heavier than teak when cut.

The funding was only to build the ships. It was the cost of administration, of forming a Navy Department of civil servants that concerned them.

44-gun USS Constitution, *still floating after over 222 years*

Halfway through the building program in 1796, The Peace Treaty of Tripoli was signed.

All work on the ships stopped.

So what do you do with six half-finished warships? It's obvious, Minister, you stick an ad on Gumtree and sell the building materials for scrap.

Fortunately, Tom Jefferson realised the second-hand value was zilch and persuaded the bean counters to let four of the ships be completed. The others were dismembered for scrap and spares. But funds were then refused to actually man the four ships and allow them to put to sea... ("Far too expensive, Minister.")

Then the Pasha of Tripoli demanded $225,000 protection money in 1801. Jefferson refused. The Pasha declared war on the US. To show he was serious, he chopped down the flagpole in the US Consul's garden. Jefferson sent his new fleet to north Africa. They defeated the Tripolitan ship *Tripoli* and blockaded their ports. Meanwhile, the US Consul, outraged at the invasion of his garden, desecration of his flagpole and the stomping on his wife's chrysanthemum beds, raised an assorted rabble of 500 mercenaries. Lead by just eight marines, they captured the garrison town of Derna. This not only demoralised the locals and Tripoli immediately surrendered. It also added a stirring line in the marines' Battle Hymn ('... to the shores of Tripoli...').

But these Barbary blokes still had not learnt that you don't mess with the new America. In

With the US Consul's wife's chrysanthemums ruined by the act of chopping down the American flagpole, this meant war...

1815, the ruler of Algeria repudiated previous peace treaties and threatened all Christians in Algeria. (There were allegedly more white Christian slaves in north Africa than any other group.) He had one brig and one frigate. The US then had ten ships just round the corner… These less than 200-foot wooden ships (which had sailed the Atlantic, bringing their own munitions and sandwiches with them) reduced Algiers to rubble in about the same time Putin's jets take to level a hospital.

After 1815, peace broke out in Europe. England and France, with no enemies on which to practise their gunnery, cruised their fleets in the Mediterranean sunshine off north Africa, just hoping for one of these local ships to try their luck against a merchantman. Any merchantman. Hey, the British would even defend a French ship now.

The Barbarian business model suffered further decline when France colonised Algeria in 1830 and Tunisia in 1881.

The locals then fell under the dubious oxymoron of French administration, but the bread and coffee improved, and they developed a wine industry which still produces reds used by airlines that most of us avoid.

In 1904, a Greek American and his son were kidnapped for a $70,000 ransom in Tangier. He had actually renounced his American citizenship 40 years before to avoid US taxes, but his kidnappers didn't know this. Neither did President Teddy Roosevelt. Otherwise, he probably would not have sent seven warships and a massive batch of marines. No talk about 'Crossing a line' then and doing nothing. The prisoners were released immediately. It was Teddy who coined the phrase 'Speak softly but carry a big stick…'

Remember that the original frigates were built to a very high specification with meticulous workmanship. The 44-gun *Constitution*, *Old Ironsides*, was launched in 1797 and is the oldest Navy ship still afloat. *Victory* was last floating on her own bottom in 1922.

So always go for that extended warranty…

Teddy Roosevelt may have had a cuddly toy named after him, but he was one tough cookie. He was the youngest ever US President at 42 when McKinley was assassinated. He tragically lost his mother of typhoid and wife in childbirth within hours of each other on Valentine's Day 1884. While on the campaign trail he made an 84-minute speech after being shot in the chest. Most pollies of today would probably pack it in if the teleprompter went on the blink. Here he is, with his Mount Rushmore teeth, speaking softly but carrying a big stick

LAWRENCE TO THE RESCUE

Creating a fast rescue launch for the RAF with mutiple future uses

You may have guessed that the RAF fitter who worked on the engines of the support craft for the Schneider Trophy (Chapter 4) was Lawrence of Arabia (T E Shaw). Quirky expands on his nautical achievements which included moving his wife's in-laws from Wolverhampton to the south coast. And just keeps dredging up more useless stuff from his schoolboy memories...

Aircraftman Shaw took burns patients out for exhilaratingly wet test drives

I find it interesting that when Colonel T E Lawrence tried to join the RAF as Aircraftman James Hume Ross in 1922, he was rejected by the recruiting pilot officer who thought it was a fictional name. This officer would know about fiction. He later wrote 99 *Biggles* adventures under the name of Captain W E Johns. The 'Captain' was a fictional title he awarded to himself. Lawrence eventually signed on as Aircraftman Shaw.

In 1931 he saw a flying boat crash into the sea. He boarded the pinnace that chugged out to rescue the crew but, despite Lawrence reportedly diving into the sinking hull, only 3 out of the 12 were saved. He complained vociferously to the RAF brass that they needed their own fast boats and not rely on cast-off ex-Navy 'dull, stupid, heavy motorboats'.

He was not alone. At the same time, the water speed record holder, and founder of the British Powerboat Company, Hubert Scott-Payne (the hyphen was self-awarded fiction using his parents' names) had been pressing his high-speed designs for a 'mile-a-minute navy' (60mph) to the Admiralty. While he was waiting for their Lordships to make up their minds, he offered to build fast 35-foot rescue launches for the RAF. They fancied 40 foot. They compromised at 37' 6".

But from where could they source 100hp light-weight engines in the UK? Boat engines from Brooke Marine in Lowestoft (one of the few suitable marine engine makers of the time) were tried and rejected. So to get a *marine* engine, Lawrence went to the heart of the industrial Midlands, as far from the sea as you can get... possibly on one of the seven hand-made Brough Superior motorcycles he owned... (Sadly, he did not collect his eighth; he was killed in 1935 riding his 1929 SS100

The Lagonda Rapide: From all angles, one of the most rakish-looking cars of the period.

with the same 50bhp JAP engine that pulled the Morgan three wheelers along at over 100mph...)

Henry Meadows in Wolverhampton made sports car engines. His 1½ litre powered the chain-driven Frazer Nash and the 4½ was used by Invictor and Lagonda. (In 1935, a private entry Lagonda Rapide, surely one of the most rakish looking cars of the golden age, powered by the almost indestructible Meadows engine won Le Mans averaging 78.88mph despite drinking nearly all its own sump oil on the last laps.)

Wolverhampton made everything then. It had innovative and educated engineers and a highly skilled workforce. They manufactured products from toilet bowls to tank engines, from jelly to jets. (Wolverhampton still makes stuff today, despite all the empty factories and the highest percentage of shuttered shop fronts in Britain (26%). They make curry. The plethora of balti outlets is why some refer to the place as the commercial heartland of Bangladesh.)

Lawrence needed these engines to be marinised, installed and maintained by specialists. Meadows engineers were asked if they would consider leaving the soot-stained suburbs of Wolverhampton and move to Hythe on the bracing banks of the Solent. My wife's late husband's father, Bob, thought he could survive this. He became project manager at the British Powerboat Company. They modified the engines to run at an angle of 17 degrees, without a radiator, water cooling only, to develop a constant, reliable 100bhp. Except for the US-owned Vauxhall and Ford, British cars all came with electrics supplied by the 'Prince of Darkness' (the term of derision used by motorists for Lucas electrical products). This must have been an additional headache in a marine environment.

Bob told the family that he was working with this enthusiastic little RAF chap, Shaw, who had digs with Mrs Biddlecombe at Myrtle Cottage in St Johns Street, Hythe. Shaw was only 5'5". Peter O'Toole was a nearly a foot taller than the character he played as Lawrence of Arabia.

Shaw had friends in the Air Force and a few had been burnt in accidents. He took them out for exhilaratingly wet test rides in the launches believing that the salt spray would be good for their burns. He was dead right. The New Zealand doctor Archie McIndoe who became the RAF burns specialist during the war confirmed this from Channel-ditched pilots in World War Two. He introduced saline baths which became a standard treatment for burns victims.

A certain US Air Force Captain (Clark Gable)

Incidentally, his burns unit was critically short of medical supplies with the war-time shortages. A USAF Captain from a nearby base visited the unit; he had experienced minor plastic surgery himself and was an entertaining and popular visitor among the patients. He asked McIndoe for a list of what he needed. They arrived shortly afterwards.

The visitor had clout with the US President who had ordered him to stay out of active service and keep selling war bonds. His wife had just died while returning from a successful bonds tour… Clark Gable was a hero off the screen as well as on.

The RAF rescue boats had chine hulls which were simple to build with a double skin bottom and single diagonal-planked seam-battened sides. They could reach 29 knots (33mph) with two Meadows engines. Later versions were extended to 43' x 13'0" x 3'6". One of these was used in the fifties to ply between Guernsey and Herm in the Channel Islands. As we ripped across the three-mile Little Russell Channel, my father said, "This has to be 40mph!" It certainly felt like it, but the skipper confirmed it was only 17 knots (20mph) with the two Perkins SM6 120hp diesels. Incredibly, he told us these only sipped 3gph.

Once the RAF started taking delivery of these fast seaworthy boats, they found a myriad of uses for them. They also became known as seaplane tenders. BOAC used them for passengers on their imperial flying boats.

I remember one, bought out of service in 1956 but retained her RAF paint job and kept at Stourport on the River Severn. Number 441, an easy number to paint and maintain. The owner kept her for over 50 years until he was in his nineties and used to exercise the big ends on holidays down the Bristol Channel and as far as Cornwall. Just wonderful!

She then had an eight-year rebuild by her new owners. You can see her in action on YouTube.

Looks fantastic, doesn't she?

I might have a go at building a 1:12 scale radio control model. For the younger grandsons of course, I'm far too grown up for such things.

I might have a go at building a radio control model of Lawrence's fast tenders

THE SEA DEVIL CONNECTION

The little-known story of Felix Von Luckner, the German tormentor of shipping

While in lockdown we binged on some wonderful classic films. We were particularly interested to see Lawrence of Arabia again as we had been to Jordan and seen relics of his Aquaba campaign. You may remember in the film there is an American reporter who tags along with Lawrence, in a suit and tie, and helps bring his legendary feats to the outside world. In the film he is called Jackson Bentley. The real journalist was Lowell Thomas, who filmed extensively with Lawrence then delivered a series of movie-based lectures around the world. He was an avid promoter of travel. Among his books was The Sea Devil, the story of Felix von Luckner, a copy of which was bequeathed to me 50 years ago.

I meet Lowell Thomas – we were both trying to avoid the attendant

Amazingly, I met Lowell Thomas at the Waldorf Astoria where I was based and was able to thank him for the enjoyment this book had brought me. Not as auspicious as it sounds. It was in the Gents there. We were both trying to get out without incurring the expensively excruciating bonhomie of the attendant who brushed the dandruff from his previous victim onto your collar with one hand while the other was subtly outstretched. It was said that he paid an annual fee to the hotel for his job, so lucrative were the tips.

Thomas was still broadcasting into the seventies with his well-known signing off catch phrase* – that's quite a career span from working with Lawrence 65 years before.

I am surprised that few people know the story of von Luckner, the Sea Devil, who raided Allied shipping during World War One in *Seeadler*. She was originally an American fully-rigged steel ship that, despite being a *neutral*, was seized by a German U-boat while delivering cotton to Archangel and the crew was imprisoned.

I had forgotten some of the interesting

bits until re-reading the 95-year-old book recently. Thomas' prose is straight from *The Boys Own Paper*. There's lots of: *'By Joe, let me get my pipe started and I'll tell you a tale…!'* Even Kaiser Bill apparently spoke like this. *'By thunder, you must tell me about it!'* It has more exclamation marks per square inch than a Trump Tweet. You feel you want to flick them off the page.

Felix von Luckner came from a wealthy cavalry family but didn't want to follow the family business and ran away to sea at 13, vowing not to return until he was wearing the uniform of an officer in the Kaiser's Navy.

Instead of signing on at a naval college, he joined a Russian ship as an unpaid cabin boy sailing to Australia. Off the Cape of Good Hope he was flicked overboard from a height of 90 feet while unfurling the main topsail. Despite the skipper's orders, a volunteer crew launched the lifeboat, but Felix had then disappeared in a fury of foam. The crew saw a flock of albatross circling and one bird that was stationary and struggling. It had attacked Felix and he had grabbed its claws. Thirty years later he showed Lowell Thomas the scars from its beak that saved his life. He was particularly proud of his large, damaged hands. One of his party tricks was to bend coins between his fingers.

Von Luckner grabbed the claws of the albatross that attacked him

In Australia, the runaway Count became an assistant lighthouse keeper at Cape Leeuwin, joined the Salvation Army, became a wrestler and kangaroo shooter and toured with a troupe of performing Indian Fakirs before crossing the Pacific. He made a 285-day voyage from San Francisco to Liverpool with 180 days of stores, most of which were spoiled by seawater on the way.

Most of us would have taken up farming or stamp collecting then, but he signed aboard the sailing ship *Caesarea* for a passage to New York carrying mainly chalk and 300 tons of arsenic powder. This is a very heavy cargo. They had rough North Atlantic weather with an inexperienced crew of steamship stokers and trimmers who had never been aboard a sailing ship before.

While celebrating Christmas during a lull in the strong winds, a white squall hit them on the nose, wiped out all the upper masts and smashed the helmsman to a mortally-wounded pulp. The wind increased to hurricane force and the ship took on water, the pumps were fully manned around the clock. Then the arsenic smashed through the steerage deck and many of the barrels disintegrated.

While the steamer crew hid in the fo'c'sle, the sailors tried to restow the arsenic, choking on its dust. Massive waves now broke over the stricken ship and swept the cook and his galley overboard. Luckner braced himself for the next wave between two deck timbers. The power of that wave washed six men overboard and smashed his leg into an L. The carpenter straightened it with a block and tackle and lashed a splint to it so Felix could carry on pumping.

The ship foundered and they took to the two lifeboats. The one with the mate in charge was never seen again. Felix was in the skipper's boat. After six days with hardly any food or water, they were drawing lots for who should be sacrificed to feed the others when an Italian steamer rescued them.

Von Luckner eventually returned home dressed as an officer in the Kaiser's Navy to a family that had given him up for lost. As one of the few officers who had real square rigger experience, he was given command of *Seeadler* to sail through the British blockade of Germany that eventually starved them into an armistice and go raiding Allied shipping in the Atlantic and Pacific. He did it all with only one casualty and collected passengers and crew from all the ships he sunk. He captured a French barque *Cambronne*, cut down her topmasts to slow her down and dispatched 300 of his passengers.

Von Luckner either off to meet Kaiser Bill or to audition for a German version of HMS Pinafore

He rounded The Horn and was driven so far to the south; he avoided the three ships of the Royal Navy sent to capture him. *Seeadler* sailed to Mopelia for a much-needed bottom scrape and refit. It was here von Luckner claimed the ship was driven ashore by a tsunami and wrecked. His 46 US prisoners said the ship just drifted ashore while the Germans were off having a picnic. (A modern expedition has confirmed the latter is more likely.) Von Luckner and five men sailed the 32-foot whaler 3,700 miles to Fiji, planning to capture another sailing boat and rescue his comrades. He aroused suspicion and was captured by being told a non-existent gun aboard a ferry would blow his cutter out of the water. They were imprisoned in New Zealand.

The whaler under sail, which von Luckner sailed 3,700 miles to Fiji, only to be captured and interred from which he made another daring escape

While he was away, a French ship anchored off Mopelia and was taken by the German crew. They sailed for South America but were wrecked on Easter Island and interred until the end of the war.

The captured American skipper of the *A B Johnson*, with three other seamen sailed 900 miles in the remaining ship's boat to Pago Pago to report their story to the authorities and organise a rescue of the stranded sailors from the island.

In New Zealand, von Luckner stole the prison officer's launch and used it to capture a 90-ton scow. These are flat bottomed sailing craft. He was heading for the Kermadec Isles when a New

Zealand ship pursued him, and he was back in New Zealand. There he made plans to hide in an empty tar barrel and to be pushed into the water where he had observed floating barrels were regularly picked up and hoisted aboard a small schooner. Armed with a knife, he would take over the ship, collect his mates and sail off for somewhere neutral. This adventure was scotched by the Armistice being declared.

Between the wars he became a celebrity on both sides undertaking lecture tours and a cruise around the world in his yacht. He hosted a dinner in Brisbane where a swastika appeared on the menu. The Australian Intelligence service kept an eye on the Germans on the guest list and interred most of them at the declaration of World War Two.

Von Luckner was so anti-Hitler that he wound up with a price on his head. One of his last courageous acts was to give a passport he had found in the rubble of war-torn Germany to a Jewish woman and smuggle her out of the country. After the war, he married a Swedish countess and settled there… I remember sitting in a Nairobi club reading his obituary in *Time* in April 1966 and was impressed that he received such recognition.

You can still get the book and it is available on Kindle. Give it a go.

By thunder, you will enjoy it!

A New Zealand (pronounced Nuh Z'lund by the locals) scow. Like a big pencil box with a pointy bow. Very cheaply built with not a curved line in her. Von Luckner tried to make his final escape in one of these.

* Lowell Thomas' catchphrase: "So long until tomorrow."

PLAGUE SHIPS

Influenza viruses are nothing new

At the start of the Covid epidemic in Sydney, a cruise ship with infected passengers aboard was inexplicably allowed to discharge them without medical checks. It started one of the main outbreaks in New South Wales. But it was not just this ship that allowed unchecked infected passengers ashore, this has been happening for centuries. But 600 years ago, some local officials were more cognisant and proactive towards the dangers of infection than we have seen recently in NSW. Quirky, who readers will suspect only paid attention during the History and English classes at school, rambles on...

Plague ships from the Black Sea with emaciated skeletons as crew, bringing the Black Death to Europe

Since 1887, every ship arriving in a foreign port is required to fly a yellow flag on its own which our pilot book said means 'My ship is healthy, and I require free medical pratique'. So in 1963, by a navigational error, when we arrived in the foreign port of Cherbourg instead of the British one of Alderney, we hung up a well-used yellow duster from the cabin cleaning gear. The local douanier was bemused by this and our lack of passports, he shrugged it off pointing to a local bar which took English pounds.

This is curious because for centuries, yellow was the colour associated with disease and infection. In the Middle Ages, heretics had to wear yellow clothing, this being considered the colour of hell fire. During plague epidemics, infected houses were daubed with yellow paint and their inhabitants were to wear yellow clothes. Denmark decreed the yellow flag in 1887 for their own ships to signify they were healthy, and the practice was adopted internationally.

In December 1347, the residents of Messina in Sicily watched bemused as 12 trading ships from Black Sea ports made desperately incompetent efforts to dock alongside the harbour walls. Then the reason became devastatingly clear; very few of their crews were still alive. The living were emaciated skeletons, covered with black boils that oozed blood and puss.

"I became a heretic because I just LOVED the fashion range"

"Take two Aspirin and call me in the morning. I'm off to a Halloween party."
Despite doctors trying to make their own protective gear, tragically the Black Death wiped out one third of the population

The authorities ordered the ships out of the harbour, but it was too late. Within five years, the Black Death would kill over 20 million people in Europe.

It is believed that the source from these ships originated in the Middle East and China. The symptoms were swellings of the groin, under the armpits with all the side effects of fever, aches and pains, diarrhoea and vomiting. This air-borne bacillus brought a very nasty death to a staggering one third of the population. Not only people, but farm animals were infected which further spread the disease and brought food shortages even with a reduced population.

In 1377 a system was established in Dubrovnik whereby ships were to wait for 30 days before entering port which was based on medical advice at the time. Then it appeared religion got involved by quoting all the significant traumas in the Bible were for 40 days and 40 nights. So this became the norm. As Dubrovnik was Venetian at the time and the language was Italian, this brought the word 'quarantine' into general use.

In the trading port of Venice itself, arriving ships that were suspected of carrying infection were required to send the captain ashore in a boat to the Health Magistrate's office where he would be interviewed through a glass window. Even then they were aware that infection could be spread by air droplets.

The captain had to show a health certificate from the port of loading that his crew, passengers and cargo were free of infection. If there was doubt, they would all be sent to a quarantine station for 40 days and the whole ship fumigated. An isolation hospital was established on the island of Santa Maria di Nazareth. Are you paying attention here? This was in 1423. Nearly 600 years ago.

The orange-faced guy that used to be in the White House, The Donald, the self-claimed leading authority on Coronavirus and just about everything else in the western world ('It will disappear like magic'), and whose vast daily reading is reported to devour almost the number of words on the average postal stamp, wanted to call the infection the Wuhan Virus because of its source of origin. Fine with me, but let's call the Spanish Flu by its correct name. Remember that from your extensive reading Mr POTUS? You know, the one that infected a third of the world's population and killed between 25 and 50 million people 100 years ago? Probably not. It wasn't on Fox TV.

It was called the Spanish flu by the Allies to focus on how devastating it was to the Royal Family in that neutral country during the latter days of World War One. But mainly

Kansas exports its plague

to hide the fact it was slaughtering millions in the rest of the world. So let's call it by its correct name: The Kansas Flu.

According to the Kansas Historical Society, the first recorded case was a US Army cook at Camp Funston who was hospitalised with a 104°F fever. It quickly spread through the Army base to infect 54,000 troops in one month. 1,100 were hospitalised and 38 died. A local doctor reported this to the Public Health Service, but he got the same brush off as the whistle blower in Wuhan who also became infected. Fortunately, this one survived.

So they were packed into troopships and freighters (Humphrey Bogart was a crew member on one) and sent to the jammed mud and muck filled trenches of World War One. This deadly H1N1 influenza A virus lasted two years and mutated to become the deadliest disease ever known on the face of the earth.

Not just the first wave. It changed to a more virulent and deadly strain, killing people in less than a day. Mainly fit people between 25 and 35 years of age, who woke up healthy drowned in the fluid of their own lungs by teatime. The virus was prolonged by governments not considering any social distancing, such as the Venetians had practised, because it might affect production in the munitions factories. And big Liberty Loan Drives: 200,000 people gathered in Philadelphia in September 1918 for one of these, they were told the flu had passed. Well, maybe the first wave, but two days later, every hospital bed was filled.

A third wave developed in... Australia of all places and worked its way back to Europe. So do as the medical experts tell us, not internet-only experts.

I was triple vaccinated and still became infected. If I hadn't had the jabs, you may not be reading this book.

DR TED FROM BERKELEY

Vaccines come to the rescue

I have happy childhood memories of the Berkeley ship canal. As a kid, staying at my grandfather's fishing shack on the banks of the River Severn, I watched petrol tankers and pleasure boats going down the river, through the canal from where they could go on to the rest of the world. It took 34 years to gouge the canal out of 19 miles of mud and muck using mainly private enterprise and shovels. Let's have a look at the local doctor, a country physician at the time of its building who changed the face of the world.

The history enthusiasts among you will recall Berkeley Castle which gained an unsavoury reputation for the reported particularly gruesome execution of King Edward II in 1327.

The canal was started in 1793 to bypass the most treacherous stretch of the Severn Estuary so ships would have an easier passage to Gloucester. The idea was to develop Gloucester as a port for the Severn and Avon River and the new canal links to England's heartlands. It is still a delightful way to see the country.

The canal was funded mainly by local merchants to promote this. It ran out of money with only 5½ miles being built in 1799. However, in 1817, the introduction of the Poor Employment Act was a program to deal with the mass unemployment at the end of the Napoleonic Wars and this brought government funds in to complete the project in ten years.

There are no locks along its length, just swing bridges which are manned from delightful Palladian cottages housing the keepers. It still amazes me to watch the 40-foot tides of the estuary flowing at up to eight knots around the structures of the outer sea lock. How was all this was built 250 years ago

The smooth and dashing Dr Ted kept his eye on the local milkmaids

in the swirling silt without the use of sheet metal piling?

The local medic would have been interested in watching the construction taking place as Doctor Ted was a man of science. He probably saw it from the air as he built hot air balloons and made many successful assents and one even more successful crash landing. It is said that on one of his flights he wound up ploughing the petunias of Kingscote Park Gloucestershire, much to the initial annoyance of its owner Robert Kingscote but to the delight of his daughter Catherine. We can assume that Robert forgave the aerially-intruding doctor. He had an unwed daughter on his hands who was heading for her thirties. An unmarketable commodity in those days. In 1788 he happily gave her away in marriage to the 39-year-old Dr Ted.

Dr Ted's crash landing ended up in him getting wed

While he was at school, the eight-year-old Ted was treated with variolation against smallpox. This was a process of collecting scabs from smallpox victims with only a mild case and left to dry. They were then rubbed into scratches made on the skin of the patient. It was a method developed in China and the Middle East, so patients were infected with a mild dose of smallpox. The Chinese also blew powdered smallpox scabs up patients' noses... After about four weeks, the symptoms would subside, and the patient would then be supposedly immune to further infection.

A 14-year-old Ted was apprenticed to a doctor in charming village of Chipping Sodbury in the Cotswolds and, at 21, was trained at St George's Hospital Medical School in London before returning to the country life of his beloved Gloucestershire.

Voltaire wrote at this time that 60% of the population caught smallpox and 20% of those died from it. In 1768 it was discovered by the research of Dr John Fewster that a person who had suffered cowpox would not contract the more deadly smallpox. The two ailments were related but cowpox was rarely fatal. The dashing Dr Ted kept his eye on the local milkmaid population and noticed that although their hands often became infected with cowpox blisters from constantly pulling udders, the rest of them had clear complexions unravaged by smallpox and seemed to be immune from it.

While their hands became infected, the rest of them had clear complexions

In 1796, Dr Ted tried an experiment that would change the world. Milkmaid Sarah Nelmes had contracted cowpox from a cow named Blossom. He put the puss from her infected hands into scratches he made in both arms of eight-year-old James Phipps, the son of his gardener. The same age as Dr Ted was when he was variolated – eight was considered a magic age for new medical treatments then. This produced a mild fever and uneasiness in James, but not a full-blown infection despite later injections of pure smallpox. Ted later gave the family a cottage.

It sounds risky to us now, but cowpox was not fatal unless you had a dodgy immune system. Dr Ted later treated his own 11-month-old son Robert and 22 other patients, all of whom became immune from further infections of smallpox. He named this system after its bovine source: vaccination from the Latin for cow, vacca.

Ergo: Immune from cowpox = immune from smallpox.

Some of the medical profession at the time were as receptive to medical science as the anti-vaxers are today and the Establishment was reluctant to acknowledge this breakthrough in medical science... But Dr Ted had one fervent admirer whose support finally brought him the recognition he so richly deserved.

Napoleon was so impressed by Dr Ted's work that he had all his troops vaccinated although he was at war with Britain at the time. He asked Dr Ted what reward he could give him for his life-saving achievement. The Dr asked for a prisoner exchange which was agreed as the little Corsican said, "I could not refuse anything to one of the greatest benefactors of mankind." There, put that in your CV and show it to the doubters.

His strenuous work on vaccination meant he had to give up his GP practice in Berkeley. A number of supporters, including the King, petitioned Parliament to grant him ten thousand pounds to continue his research. The Royal College of Physicians followed in 1807 and finally accepted his work and he was awarded, at the height of the Napoleonic Wars, the equivalent of a third of a battleship. He received an astonishing twenty thousand pounds to continue his research. (HMS

Victory had cost 63,176 pounds and three shillings.) That would get you a lot of cows. And milkmaids.

All this cash, but strangely, no knighthood. He received walls full of international recognition and awards including being made Physician Extraordinary to George IV. The one that gave him the greatest satisfaction was the recognition of his home village; he was made Mayor of Berkeley.

Vaccination was expanded to give immunity to dozens of other diseases, and it is reckoned Dr Ted saved over 530 million lives. The World Health Organisation (WHO) tells us that smallpox was eradicated from the face of the earth on 9 December 1979.

The last agonizing death from smallpox was in 1978. You probably think that this happened in some reeking insanitary village in the armpit of a third world dump.

Close.

It was in my hometown of Birmingham. Janet Parker was a 40-year-old medical photographer at Birmingham Medical School where they had a smallpox laboratory. It was never established how Janet contracted the fatal disease but the guilt-stricken Professor Bedson, the man in charge, went into his

You won't feel anything. It's just like a small musket ball

"That's only 2,175,333 to go sire."

garden shed and… left a bloody mess for his poor wife to find. Janet's father died from cardiac arrest at hearing of the death of his daughter. Her mother contracted a mild case of smallpox herself and missed the funerals of both her daughter and husband.

There are labs in the USA and Russia which hold samples under very tight security, we are told, in case further research becomes necessary… Yes, well I hope they have better security than they did in Birmingham. They couldn't control it then and that was before Al-Qaeda and friends set up shop in the High Street.

Unfortunately, Dr Ted lost his wife and 21-year-old son to another great killer of the age which could not be helped by his vaccinations. Despite living on the Severn Estuary which channelled mild temperate sea air up to the Vale of Evesham to create the fruit bowl of England, they both succumbed to TB, or consumption as it was then known. He did not live to see the opening of the canal that ran close by his house. He died in 1823 at 73 and James Phipps, his first vaccinated patient, attended his funeral.

His legacy lives on in the creation of the British Vaccination Acts, which banned variolation and in 1853 went on to make vaccination free and compulsory to all children within three or four months of birth. Variolation did not come with a lifetime guarantee as some patients developed smallpox after they had been treated. But still there were those who would deny their children this life saving treatment.

I found out in later life that my mother did not have me, nor my sister, vaccinated against diphtheria nor polio, two killers in the forties and fifties, because, as a child, she had heard rumours of someone who died as a result of vaccination.

But the legacy of Dr Ted, the local doctor of Berkeley, lives on and the whole world is in his debt. Fortunately, modern science came up with vaccinations against Covid. After two centuries of proof of the benefits of vaccination, there are those among us who know better. Some say vaccine deniers are a dying breed…

And there is another member of the research team that is still remembered. Blossom, the cow. Her hide hangs in grateful recognition at the St George's Hospital Medical School, the Alma Mater of Dr Edward Jenner…

Blossom, the cow, still hangs at the St George's Hospital Medical School

THE GREATEST KILLER IN NELSON'S NAVY

1.5 million still die of it worldwide

No, neither cannon balls nor scurvy were the main killers. Dr Quirky continues his lectures on the history of medical science. If it hadn't been for being self-isolating after COVID, he thinks he would have been in the UK lecturing the editorial board of The Lancet.

Nelson's Victory
Ship of the line
Keel was laid
In fifty nine
Total guns
One hundred and four
He was born the year before

J. Quirk
Form 3B.

Nelson's Victory from my school book

In the previous chapter about Dr Ted, the local GP from Berkeley, we touched on the disease that claimed his wife and 21-year-old son: consumption, as it was called then, tuberculosis or TB as it is known today. A crippling lung disease which neither alpine air nor long sea voyages could cure. With the tolls from smallpox and TB that scythed through Europe 200 years ago, it amazes me there were enough left to lose 50 million to the so-called Spanish Flu and still overrun the planet with seven billion of us.

It is generally accepted that seamen in Nelson's Navy stood a better chance of a healthier life than the nine million who were in Britain at the time, trying to keep the place going and providing enough export income to fund the war. Apart from the monotony, the Navy diet was generally considered better than the landman's at the time, chomping a whopping 5,000 calories a day. Two pounds of beef on Tuesday and Saturday and one pound of pork on Sunday and Thursday. It certainly had a higher proportion of meat than most of the population.

And it came with free booze. Originally this had been a gallon of beer. Yes, eight pints a day. I couldn't have managed that over a long weekend even in my prime. But it was safer to drink than the ship's water. But even beer went off in the tropics and was replaced by half a pint of spirits. Because Britain had sugar plantations in the West Indies, the industrial waste became rum. And it was cheap. That's why it became the Navy's choice tipple. This was watered down 1:4 in the 1740s but even so, most of the sailors spent their lives half pissed. The Lords of the Admiralty continued this until 1970 when they thought that if you would fail a breathalyser test after the 11:00am tot and couldn't drive a car, you really shouldn't be driving a submarine.

THE FASTEST KNIFE IN THE OR

If you were going to have a limb amputated without anaesthetic in the 19th century, you would want it to be over as soon as possible, and then Dr Robert Liston was your man. He had a sort of production line going and perfected his speed in amputation to minimise shock to the patient and to cover as great a workload among the suffering as he could in a working day. Despite this, he had a low fatality rate of 1-in-10 when 1-in-4 was the going rate. The *Guinness Book of Records* was not around to record his personal best of two and a half minutes, including sewing up, when he amputated a patient's leg and the fingers of the assistant who was holding him down. While rapidly changing knives, he accidently caught a spectator's coat who thought he had been stabbed and promptly died from a heart attack. The patient and assistant later succumbed to infection. This 300% casualty rate from one op obviously detracted from his overall batting average. He became the first surgeon in the UK to use ether as an anaesthetic. Good for the patients but maybe not for the staff and spectators when the operating theatres were lit by gas lamps... Boom!

The world's fastest amputator, Dr Robert Liston, from a portrait by Samuel John Stump (I don't make this stuff up!)

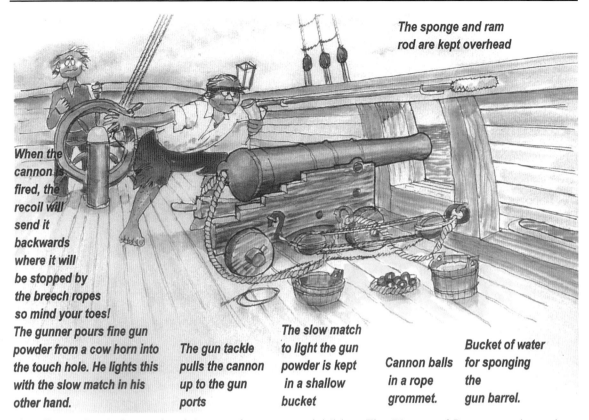

The sponge and ram rod are kept overhead

When the cannon is fired, the recoil will send it backwards where it will be stopped by the breech ropes so mind your toes!

The gunner pours fine gun powder from a cow horn into the touch hole. He lights this with the slow match in his other hand.

The gun tackle pulls the cannon up to the gun ports

The slow match to light the gun powder is kept in a shallow bucket

Cannon balls in a rope grommet.

Bucket of water for sponging the gun barrel.

This illustration is from a book I wrote for my grandchildren The Pirates of Patonga, *where they are captured but engineer their own escape and shows how a cannon works*

While smallpox vaccinations were compulsory in Napoleon's army, it was voluntary in the Royal Navy and many declined 'for religious reasons'. Scurvy had been partly brought under control after Navy doctor James Lind's successful experiments using lemons on his patients. The Navy only took 42 years to accept it in 1795 and it was only at the urging of other naval doctors who had read Lind's work.

Captain Cook you will remember had similar success with sauerkraut and malt. I remember enjoying the malt to take away the taste of the cod liver oil we war-time kids were given, together with sun lamp exposure to replace sunlight to give us vitamin D. I think sunshine was on ration then too.

The antiscorbutic power of lemons was reduced by storage and boiling, which was used as method used to make juice. Plantations were set up in the West Indies to grow limes. Because they were more acidic it was wrongly thought they were the better fruit. In fact, limes have only 29.1mg of Vitamin C per 100 grams versus 53 for lemons. See? Homework doesn't stop when you leave school.

OK, so they had smallpox and scurvy sort of under control, apart from yellow fever, what's next? How about cannon balls? Actually no. Despite Britain having over 150 ships of the line and being at war with France and just about everybody else for over two decades, very few of her sailors saw more than one sea battle despite what we read in Forrester and O'Brien where they seem to occur every few pages.

The French naval museum in Paris claims loads of victorious French naval victories that did not appear in my history books. But then, that museum had never heard of Trafalgar.

The Royal Navy's ships spent most of their time on patrol, bottling up the French and Spanish Fleets so they could not leave port and actually get into combat. Nelson famously said, "Harbours rot ships and men" meaning that their lack of sea-going practice with ship handling and gunnery gave the Royal Navy the edge. A gun crew of six to eight could fire three shots from their heavy guns every five minutes, the French and Spanish could only manage one pop gun eight-pounder every four minutes. They probably stopped for lunch.

Being in the Navy was described as like being in jail with the added attraction of being drowned, so what else could kill you?

Drowning, or being lost at sea or wrecked claimed about 16% of them. Just over 6% died in battle, or more likely on the surgeon's table (less than one man a day). Mainly by flying splinters as the oaken ships pounded themselves to pieces. (Dudley Pope's figures of 1875 casualties are only for six sea battles.) Those are the deaths. It is amazing what trauma people can survive and rise above a handicap. My grandmother lost an arm in an industrial accident during the war. She carried it to the first aid station where everybody except her fainted. She wore a hook after that and took up needlework.

This leaves an astonishing 78% being felled by sickness. But if scurvy and smallpox were controlled, what was left? There was typhus, imported when the jails were emptied to swell the crews, and there was yellow jack. But one that might surprise you that we associate more with 19th century drawing rooms than a ship of the line…

The dreaded consumption, mate.

Up until then, it had killed one-in-seven people that ever lived.

Even with all that bracing sea air, the TB bacteria hung in the dark fetid quarters,

Swooning poets going down with the white disease

spreading mainly from lungs to lungs in the ships where hundreds of men lived and worked for up to two years at a time. The space allowed for hammocks was 18 inches even in my day.

We think of consumption as a prevalent ailment of the upper leisured classes, especially poets and writers, going dead white and swooning away, clasping lace hankies to their foreheads. Indeed, it was known as The White Disease or The Romantic Disease claiming Keats at 25, Henry David Thoreau at 44, Emily Bronte at 30. But history does not include the millions of ordinary working-class people crammed into the slums of the Industrial Revolution. Escaping from these foul conditions, sailors brought the infection aboard their ships. In the US, Doc Holliday, the dentist turned gambler and gunslinger, survived being shot at the gunfight at the OK Corral but died from TB in the high clear air of Colorado at 36. His long-term girlfriend, the charmingly named but quite attractive Hungarian-born hooker, Big Nose Kate, did not contract it from him and died at 91, just three weeks before I was born. Remarkable, when it claimed all four Bronte sisters and their brother living in that one rectory.

Treatment against TB was only developed in 1921 when an oral preparation was proven successful. It was in 1943 that Selman Waksman discovered streptomycin which was tried on the first human patient in 1949. However, there was no immediate widespread vaccination against TB in children as there was for smallpox.

But I probably already had it by then…

There were 800 of us at our grammar school and in 1954 we were all lined up and vaccinated in the arm. They probably used the same needle for all of us back then. They certainly did at primary school where it sat in a dish of alcohol. A week later, everybody came up with an itching lump at the site of the vaccination, except for four of us. We were just told to sit in the corridor while the other 796 (the school was big on teaching sums) were vaccinated again. We four thought we were isolated because we were infected and were all going to die. We were all trying to be brave, sitting on Death Row with the prospect of an early demise at 13. Then a white coat with squeaky shoes approached us with a needle. We four had natural immunity he said, and he wanted to take samples to help with a vaccine. **Why didn't you tell us???**

It was only recently after a chest x-ray that my doctor told me I had been infected with TB as a youngster. Researching this article has given me a clue on how I might have contracted it. When staying at my grandfather's riverside fishing shack I used to collect warm unpasteurised milk from the farmer in a jug, straight from the cow… I am not alone. Despite the school only having a 0.5% infection rate (see, I did pay some attention during sums), the World Health Organisation says over 10 million people fall ill with TB every year and 1.5 million die, making it the

Quirky on death row

world's most infectious killer. Amazingly, one quarter of the world's population is infected with TB bacteria, but only 5-15% will fall ill with the disease. Just like at school.

If you catch it, a long sea voyage will not cure it and, as we have recently seen, the internal air conditioning of cruise ships ensures that what goes around comes around. Early treatments were quite lengthy, I knew someone whose TB lung in the fifties required a full year in bed. Modern antibiotics will kill the infection in six to nine months.

So, at the end of *The Hound of the Baskervilles*, when Sir Henry is advised to take a long sea voyage to repair his health, there should have been one proviso: Just stay on deck.

Don't go below.

Quirky experiments with centrifugal force while bringing home the unpasteurised milk which may have given him TB

Sir Henry Baskerville recovers his health on deck

MIMI & *TOUTOU* GO FORTH

Taking your trailer-sailer to the coast will never seem so bad

Quirky recalls an incredible adventure of World War One in east Africa that unfortunately escaped being made into one of those British black and white comedies...

I recently lost a dear mate to the big C.

Howard (pronounced 'Hard' in his RAF war-time officer's voice) was the dashing bush pilot who served up Pimms with the kick of aviation octane fuel. You could fly a Lancaster bomber on the ones he made.

I met him in the Long Bar of Nairobi's New Stanley Hotel over 50 years ago. We had the only two MGAs in Nairobi which could frequently be seen lurking outside the nurse's home at Nairobi Hospital.

We actually became related. He was later my son's father-in-law.

One of his last Christmas gifts to me was a book which is a constant reminder of those *Boy's Own Paper* adventures we shared in east Africa in those dying days of Empire.

If Hard had been born 60 years earlier, I am sure he would have been part of this.

The land-based nautical adventure

Mimi and Toutou Go Forth by Giles Foden (Last King of Scotland) is just one of a series of unbelievable tales of World War One in east Africa. The Germans ruled Tanganyika with an iron jackboot. (After 1962, Tanganyika + Zanzibar = Tanzania.) And that included Lake Tanganyika, the longest lake in the world which bordered on the colonial possessions of various allies on the western shores.

To patrol what they considered their own private sea, the Germans built a fleet of iron steamers, up to 1,200 tons in the Fatherland, and then took them apart into handy pieces (maximum 27 kilos per porter; that's the weight of my 9.8 Tohatsu outboard motor and I struggle to get that on and off) which were shipped out and carried over mountains and IKEA-ed together on the lake shore. With the lake's freshwater for the boilers and Africa's tropical forests for fuel, they just about

IKEA shipbuilding on the shore of Lake Tanganyika

had perpetual motion.

So what was the British response to this challenge to their African possessions? Well, in a story that Ealing Studios sadly overlooked, John Lee, a white hunter from east Africa showed up at the Admiralty in 1915, probably in Khakis and a pith helmet. He had a proposal too bizarre for a serious adventure film. It was adopted by the Admiralty but sadly, it was not turned into one of those black and white Ealing comedies of the fifties and sixties.

Lee proposed that a couple of light gunboats be sent out overland to Lake Tanganyika to harass and sink the German threat.

Film buffs can imagine their own cast here, but I see Robert Morley in full naval uniform attending the trials of two 40-foot launches that Thorneycroft were building on the Thames for the Greek Air Force and were commandeered by the Royal Navy. They could reach nearly 20 knots with their two 100hp petrol engines. The Admiralty added a three-pounder to the foredeck. However, when it was test fired, both gun and gunner were blown backwards into the Thames and shattered a number of the boat's structural frames which caused major leaks. "Well, there may be a few teething problems to be sorted out" observes an otherwise enthusiastic Morley waddling off towards the nearest gin and tonic.

To command this land-based naval expedition, their Lordships selected an eccentric failure. Through a series of blunders of his own making, the 39-year-old Geoffrey Spicer-Simson was the oldest lieutenant commander in the Royal Navy. (He later turned out to be a coward right up there with the *Goon Show*'s Major Bloodknock.) In a perfect role for Terry Thomas, the goateed self-basting S-S was covered in bizarre tattoos of wildlife. He also carried out the entire campaign in 'skirts' that were made by his wife. Probably kikoys that we wore on the east African coast and are cooler than shorts. The natives called him Lord Bellycloth. It is not recorded what his 28 Royal Navy men called him.

Those of us who think twice about trailing the boat 100 miles loaded with a couple of insulated drinks coolers and petrol cans, will marvel that to surprise the Germans, these two 40-foot boats, hundreds of gallons of

John Lee had a cunning plan

petrol, spares, two steam tractors, ammunition and packed lunches for a few thousand porters were to be sent overland, a distance of over 1,600 miles, 3,000 kilometres, to reach this *east African* lake... from South Africa.

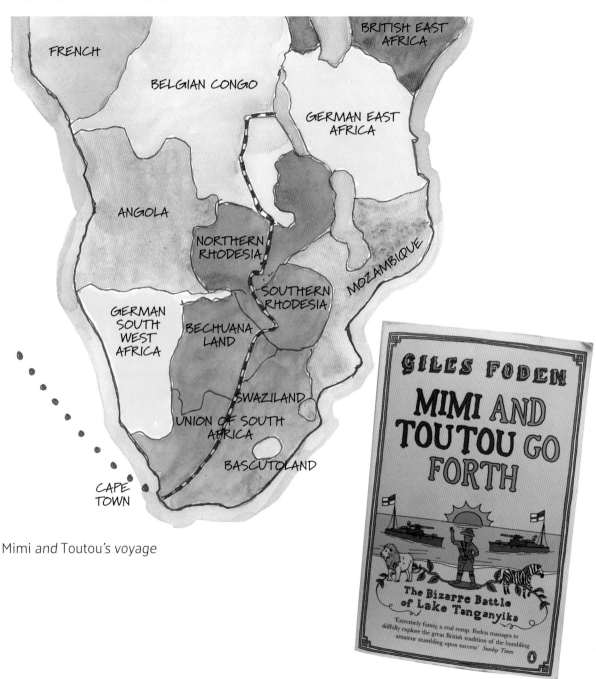

Mimi and Toutou's voyage

The two launches, called *Mimi and Toutou* ('cat' and 'dog' in French children's slang), were shipped to Cape Town, popped onto a train and sent north to Elizabethville in the Belgian Congo, a mere 2,800 kilometres. From here they were hauled 160 kilometres over 2,000-metre mountains, to be loaded onto a narrow-gauge railway heading towards the lake.

Finally, the boats would be floating again, using eastward flowing tributaries. This 160k mountaineering trip took six weeks and involved building over 150 bridges. The two steam tractors were too heavy for these steep muddy conditions and masses of South African oxen were recruited. Then the rivers were found to be too shallow to float the launches so, no doubt fingering through the *Yellow Pages* again, they sourced a few thousand barrels to build rafts to float the whole expedition down to the lake.

I don't want to spoil the ending for you, but no film script writer would ever dream up such a credibility-stretching finale. Not even the one who doctored the ending of C S Forrester's *African Queen*. So get the book. Also imagine who would have played in it if it had been made into a film. I see 'Hard' here as an extra, losing his temper with a bogged down steam tractor, perhaps beating it with a Cleesian twig, and swearing at it in Swahili.

He was very good at that.

Hard berating a steam tractor with a Cleesian stick

OFF TO D-DAY IN A FOUR POSTER

Navigating the channels in North Brittany won't seem so difficult again

Quirky reflects on the skill and bravery of those who went ahead to prepare the beaches for the Normandy landings. He recalls one enigmatic naval officer who commanded an unusual ship. He was entrusted with the top-secret instructions for Operation Neptune, for the Normandy landings, the initial part of Operation Overlord, the Allied invasion of north-west Europe. This was a dangerous task from which he doubted he would return. The orders were to be destroyed after reading...

Fully expecting to be blown to bits at any moment

Readers of the book *Foul Bottoms* may recall the Other Crew Member (OCM). The delightful young lady whose underwear nearly sank a GRP motor-sailer... No, not telling, you will have to read all about it.

One of her many attractions was a naval officer father who was one of life's most delightful characters. Like a more friendly version of James Robertson Justice who seemed to play the father of every British screen comedy heroine in those days.

A dashing, bearded naval officer from central casting, the RNVR Lieutenant Commander, as he finished up, was an Ulsterman who raised the Union Jack on a flagpole in his English front garden every morning and saluted it. Something you probably wouldn't be allowed to do in the UK today. You might offend someone.

The family house was a miniature Greenwich Museum of nautical memorabilia, stacked with photos, pictures and ship models. There was one slender model of a turn-of-the-century steam yacht, so fine and elegant that it looked as if it could pass through water without getting wet or leaving a wake. He built this model of the ship in which he arrived at the shores of Normandy, just before the invasion.

Alexander North Hardy was born in a waterfront house in Northern Ireland to a seafaring family. Eager to go to sea, he joined the Belfast Steamship Company. But there was a recession on, and jobs were scarce. So they gave him an office job.

In Birmingham.

He was saved from dying of boredom, he said, by a stroke of luck. World War Two was declared. There was no conscription in Northern Ireland, but he signed on in the Royal Navy. At first, he went back to his old company, manning guns on the now armed Belfast Steamship Company ferries. He was later sent to HMS *King Alfred*, a leisure centre

A bearded dashing naval officer from central casting

converted to a 'stone frigate' training base which prepared him for the dangerous and chilly task of convoy duty to Newfoundland. He was rewarded with his own ship. After the cramped huddled hardship of convoy ships, she was quite a change.

The elegant 60-metre, 14-knot steam yacht, SS *Dolaura*, renamed *Valena*, had been built in Scotland in 1908 for a Canadian lumber baron. Her original owner showed her to the Kaiser whom he met on a cruise to Kiel. He was duly impressed and ordered a similar, but larger, one to be built in Germany.

As the owner's son rushed from Canada to England to sign up for World War One, he was lost aboard the *Lusitania*. Ironically, she was sunk on the Kaiser's orders.

The father sold *Valena* as he felt she was haunted by the ghost of his late son. Hardy confirmed many inexplicable events aboard, particularly footsteps echoing from an empty bridge which unnerved his crew.

With remarkable foresight, the Admiralty could see the coming conflict with Germany and obtained several ships to be converted for naval duties. They bought SS *Valena* and refitted her as a minesweeper; just one month before the outbreak of war.

They put the bowsprit into storage but left the elegant clipper bow and painted her battleship grey. The interior was gutted and refitted to suit naval service, but time was short, so the owner's quarters were left for use by the captain. This was in the style preferred by turn of the century millionaire industrialists or today's dictators. This included a magnificently carved four-poster with an ensuite marble bathroom. The tub was specially cast by Royal Doulton with the obligatory gold-plated fittings.

Young Lieutenant Hardy patrolled the Irish Sea in this luxury on minesweeping duties. There was a real worry at the time that neutral, but mainly anti-British, Ireland was being used as base by German submarines.

In 1944, he received secret orders for Operation Neptune telling him that he would be starting D-Day one day ahead of the invasion as one of the many minesweepers (estimates vary from 98 to 255), that had to clear German mines from the sea up to ten miles out from the Normandy beaches.

Inside this defensive barrage was a mine-free channel used by the Kriegsmarine. But inshore from that was heavily mined to the beaches. *Valena* and other minesweepers had to cut clear channels though the outer minefield so that 120 frogmen could go in and tackle the inshore mines. He was given from 08:00pm on 5 June until 05:00am the next morning to complete the task. All in nine hours.

If you have ever had a problem rafting up with your boating mates in a cross wind, think about this: 350 ships, all stringing paravanes and other devices, clearing mines, at night, in Force 5 conditions ten miles off a lee shore full of German defences, while maintaining radio silence. Very demanding seamanship for someone who, only four years earlier, was commanding a desk in Birmingham.

The mines had to be cleared in one go, immediately before the invasion as sweeping for mines often meant blowing them up. And you did not want to disturb the German's beauty sleep with a series of continuous cracker nights. It might also have given them a clue that there would be an extra 156,000 for tea on 6 June.

Many minesweepers were built of wood so that they could sneak up undetected on magnetic mines. Some steel ships had degaussing belts added to neutralise their magnetic signature by running an electro-magnetic charge through a coil around the ship. *Valena* was just 900 tons of elegant iron, with the magnetic subtlety of Pittsburgh, but she did have that catwalk model skinny hull which could slide through the water with barely a ripple to be picked up by pressure-sensing mines. Also, her luxury yacht silent steam engines designed not to disturb her owner's hangovers gave her a chance against the acoustic sensing mines. But Hardy thought he had even less chance than the proper minesweepers of surviving this action. Without alluding to the operation, he wrote a passionate letter to his wife and young daughter, in case he did not come back. It reached her unscathed through the censor.

Valena, 900 tons of elegant iron with the magnetic subtlety of Pittsburgh

Valena and her consorts swept narrow, mine-free safe passages for the 7,000-ship invasion fleet. These were as little as 400 yards wide in places, they were buoyed with coded signals and the safe channels expanded. *Valena* towed hawsers strung between other ships to trawl mines up from the seabed.

At the same time, small inshore boats delivered frogmen into the shallows which were defended with massive steel frames, designed to pierce any ship's bottom, all heavily mined. These 120 frogmen not only cleared an astonishing 2,500 obstacles under German batteries but laid the obstructions flat for the landing craft to hit the beaches.

In later years, while yarning in his soft Ulster lilt, North Hardy would later play down his role as being just a cog in a very well-oiled machine. He praised others and pulled out strings of coastal photographs, pasted together showing the length of the invasion beaches. These were daringly taken by frogmen delivered by submarines to build up a complete picture of the invasion sites. "We knew exactly where we were, thanks to these."

Not only did the Allies have a photographic record, but shore parties landed on the beach in secret and took sand and soil samples to determine the bearing suitability and the parking arrangements for the 50,000 vehicles that would be landed. How did they get through the minefields to do this? Only in 1974 did we learn that the British Bletchley Park boffins had broken the German codes. They must have known the narrow channels the Kriegsmarine used.

But the biggest secret only came to light after Hardy passed away at the age of 70 and his daughter's house caught fire. The sun came through one of those 'antique' glass panels and ignited a rug. In a panic to rescue the family treasures, an inch-thick book was discovered. It is believed to be one of a very few remaining copies of the secret invasion plans for D-Day, Operation Neptune. It was to be destroyed by burning after reading… but

as a non-smoker, he did not have a light at the time.

"That was quite a nerve-wracking night before D-Day," reflected the HMS *Valena* captain. "So much and so many depended on us doing a good job and getting every mine. While everyone else was enduring unimaginable hardship, I remember squatting in the marble splendour of my private bathroom, fully expecting to be blown to bits at any moment; I thought if it happens now, I will be just like Oscar Wilde. It is said that he was fading away in a lavish hotel in Paris, with constant culinary delights being donated by an adoring manager. Oscar gazed around at the magnificent suite and said, 'I am dying beyond my means'."

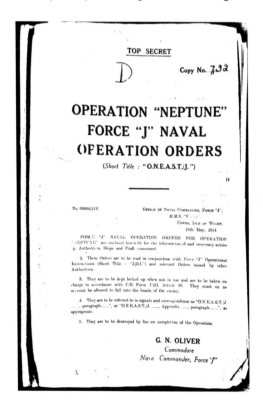

APPENDIX 'E' ANNEXE 1
NAVAL ASSAULT W/T ORGANIZATION 'Z'
(TO BE ASSUMED AT ABOUT D-12)

	BROADCAST C.N.	S.N.	ETF AUXILIARY / PORT WAVE	ADMIRALS WAVE	HOME M/F	PORTSMOUTH PORT WAVE	CHANNEL SHIP SHORE CALLING WAVE	PATROL WAVE	CONVOY R/T	JOINT FORCE BVCAST	COMMON SECTOR LANDING	NITON R/T BVCAST	B.A.N.S. VHF SPECIAL	UNLOADING WAVE	NAVAL BEACH RADAR	NAVAL SHORE	ETF REAR LINK ADMIN	ETF WHF R/T	REMARKS
PORTSMOUTH C.H.Q.	C	C	R	C	R	C	C	C	R			C							EXTRACTS ONLY OF WATCHES KEPT
N.C.E.T.F.	R	R	C	C	T	R	T	C			R°E				EXTRACTS ONLY OF WATCHES KEPT
FLAG OFFICER FORCE 'S' / COMMODORE FORCE 'G'	R	R	C	C	T	R		CW		C					CA		EXTRACTS ONLY OF WATCHES KEPT
CAPTAINS NORTHBOUND / SOUTHBOUND SAILINGS	R	R	C	C	T					R°E				EXTRACTS ONLY OF WATCHES K
ESCORTS MAJOR WAR VESSELS	R		CSE		T	CSP	T		CL°	R°E
" COASTAL FORCES EXCEPT M.L.'s			GE			GP		GE	R°E
" M.L.'s & MINOR WAR VESSELS								CL°
INDEPENDENT L.S.T. (WHITE ENSIGN)	R		CE		CP	T		CW	R°E
" L.S.T.			GE		GP	T		CW	R°E	CW	RL°
SHUTTLE SERVICE GROUPS			GE		GP	T			CW	RG
PATROLS - MAJOR WAR VESSELS	R		C		T			RL°
" A/S TRAWLERS COASTAL FORCES						C		RL°
OTHER MAJOR WAR VESSELS IN E.T.F. AREA	R		C			T		R°E
OTHER MAJOR LANDING CRAFT IN E.T.F. AREA								RL°E
F.O.B.A.A.	R	C	C	CW			C	RL°			EXTRACTS ONLY OF WATCHE
S.O.A.G	R			C			RC°E	C		CA	CA
B.A.N.J	R	R°	C				RC°E	C	C	CA		EXTRACTS O OF WATCHES
M.B.S.S.							C	C		C
P.F.C.O.							RL°		C	CB
S.O.F.C.							RL°		C	CA
S.O.F.B.							RL°		C	CB
M.T. SHIPS.							RC°E		CA
STORE SHIPS.							RC°E		CA

The top-secret invasion plans, to be destroyed after reading. You would have to be a Bletchley Park boffin to decode the hand-written instructions

THOSE MAGNIFICENT MERLINS

The engines that powered 'the few' now do the same for motorboats in Australia

As the night of 14 September ebbed into the 15th my brain woke up, stood to attention, saluted and reminded me this is the anniversary of Battle of Britain Day. It poured out the following diatribe. I can take little credit for writing it. It was like taking astral dictation. I thought we should mention this special day before the BBC and others tell us we can't, because it might upset the Germans. Just like that episode of *Fawlty Towers*.

"Runs rough at about 1,200rpm. Just take a quick look at it before the next sortie."

On Sunday 15 September 1940, the Luftwaffe launched their largest bombing attack of the war on the UK. This required virtually the entirety of the RAF fighter command being airborne in defence. The main fighters, the Hurricanes and Spitfires, were powered by the Rolls Royce Merlin engine.

Spitfire and Hurricane, powered by the Rolls Royce Merlin engine

Back in the thirties, three companies ignored the archaic whims of the Air Ministry Humphrey Applebys and designed what they thought future aviation would require for the forthcoming war with Germany. The Ministry was still issuing specifications for the fabric-covered Gloucester Gladiator biplanes as the front-line fighter of 1936, remember (see Chapter 4).

Sydney Camm quickly modified his successful biplane designs to become the sturdy easy-to-build and repair Hawker Hurricane which downed over 70% of the Luftwaffe hit during the Battle of Britain; Reg Mitchell drove himself to an early grave creating the technologically superior and more glamorous Spitfire; and Rolls Royce used shareholders' money to design and develop the initially troublesome, but eventually utterly reliable workhorse of the war, the 27-litre V12 supercharged Merlin engine.

Thank heavens they did.

The Merlin is a massive seven-feet-four-inch long (2.33m) chunk of sculptured aluminium and they cost two thousand pounds each in 1940. My father took me to see one and said "Imagine you are working in a garage, grinding valves in an Austin Seven. Then the war comes, and you are in the RAF. A pilot lands his Spitfire and says his engine is coughing a bit at 1,500rpm; can you take a look at it before he goes back up again? Where would you start? And where would you find people skilled enough to build the most advanced fighter of the day?"

Let me introduce you to one of them.

Dorothy was a beautiful 18-year-old Shropshire cinema usherette when she arrived on my parents' doorstep a few days after me. She had been billeted on us to work at Castle Bromwich in B Block, the massive building created for Spitfire manufacture. The computer-free management and training of World War Two still amazes me. Here was a teenage girl, obviously not skilled in metal work, building the most technically advanced aircraft of the age.

She worked nights solidly for four years of her youth, but always made time to read me bedtime stories in her honeyed contralto voice before going to work. I remember how thrilled my father was when she asked him to give her away when she was married from our house. She married a farmer who my mother always called 'the handsomest man in England'. And just about the nicest. We stayed in contact until Dorothy sadly passed away at 97.

Merlins also powered the Lancaster, Halifax, Mustang and Mosquito aircraft, but there seems to be a misunderstanding about their marine use. They were modified and de-tuned to power the Cromwell and Centurion tanks plus a load of others I hadn't heard of. These engines inhale a lot of air; the volume of a double decker bus *every minute*. No problems with an aircraft, there's lots of it up there, but it involves a bit of ducting in a marine application.

The owner and driving force of the British Power Boat Company, Hubert Scott hyphen Paine, saw the new Merlin as the perfect engine for his new fast designs to replace the Napier Lions left over from World War One. He popped a couple into a prototype PT boat he was hoping to sell to the Americans.

Packard built the Merlin aero engine in the US for the RAF and the Mustang under licence after Henry Ford turned it down saying it would be bad for business after Hitler won the war. It was a popular thought that the engine was 'dumbed down' for US mass production. The opposite was true. Rolls had always been the Saville Row of handmade engineering with a factory full of craftsmen who could fit a small production number of engines together with tolerances to Rolls Royce standards. This meant there could be slight differences in engines and parts may not be interchangeable. Packard, and Ford in the UK, modified the Merlin for mass production with *finer* tolerances than Rolls, so that all parts would be standardised and could be swapped around with other engines. You didn't have to know the engine number or look up the owner in *Debretts*

One of the skilled engineers building spitfires reads me a bedtime story

when grabbing a box of spares.

But the Packard *marine* engine was not a Merlin, although it was built with input from British engineers. It was designed for US PT boats and used in all British marine applications during the war.

I had the privilege of knowing Commander Michael Parker in his later years; he was the Royal Equerry and Prince Philip's best mate. While threading his Subaru through Melbourne, the three-times-married mariner recounted some of the 'fun times' of his war in his wonderful English actor's voice.

"So we set orf for neutral Sweden in an MTB with a pair of Ford V8s burbling along at maybe eight knots. Dodging the shipping and German patrols. Sneaked into port, shot six tons of Swedish ball bearings into our hold and went home. We used the three Packard engines. Brilliant! Bashing along at over 40 knots at night in a North Sea chop. We used to slow down a little to let the German E-boats catch up, just to encourage them, y'know. Then we would hit the throttles and leave them in our wake."

History records that the wooden 107-foot E-boats with three 1,320hp diesels could achieve 43 knots and were reportedly better sea boats with a longer range.

Not according to the Commander. "With our Packards and lighter, soft-chined boats, the Germans had nothing to touch us. We carried a couple of thousand gallons of petrol, so you tried not get hit and stayed just out of range. Wonderful sport. Better than foxhunting." Interesting comment from the fox outrunning the E-boat hounds.

Dave, one of the most talented engineers I have ever met, owns a hydroplane with a Merlin engine among his collection of 20 motorboats. It regularly hits 170mph (273.5kph) when he is exercising the big ends on the Hawkesbury River here in NSW. This amazing boat was designed and built by a young engineering student who was about 19-20 at the time. The engine was pulled from a Mark IX Spitfire and cost 120 pounds. How do you go about servicing an engine like that? Dave fortunately met an equally gifted ex RAAF engineer who had worked on them during the war. He was a flight engineer on Lancaster bombers who also served as the upper mid gunner. They were limited to 30 'tours' as the fatality rate in Bomber Command was an astonishing 46%. Despite that, this hero volunteered for more, managed to chalk up 120 missions and scored the only documented downing of a Messerschmitt ME 262 jet fighter from a bomber.

You would think that after the war he would have wanted to get away from six years of having Merlins throbbing in his ears. Not quite. He missed their music, he said. Back in Australia, he saw an abandoned Lincoln bomber at a local airfield. He bought all four Merlins and took them home to put into speedboats.

But that is another story.

Out running the E-boats with Packard engines

THE NAVY GOES TO LAKE TURKANA

Sailors are resourceful, but replacing a broken rudder pintles with hippo teeth takes some beating

Quirky salutes some very tough and resourceful pioneers in old Kenya, even though some of the administrators were inept.

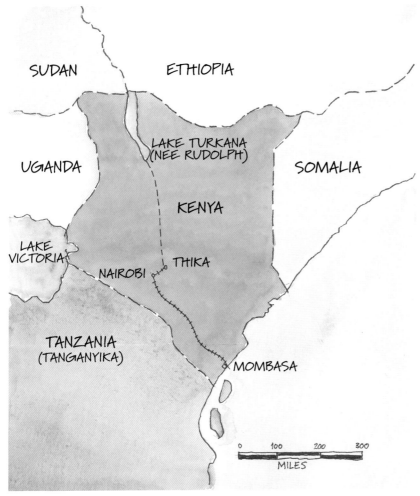

SUDAN

ETHIOPIA

UGANDA

LAKE TURKANA
(NEE RUDOLPH)

SOMALIA

KENYA

LAKE
VICTORIA

THIKA

NAIROBI

TANZANIA
(TANGANYIKA)

MOMBASA

0   100   200   300
MILES

How the Navy got to Lake Turkana

When some people hear I spent a near decade in east Africa, they feel compelled to unload all their grievances about the British Colonial system on me.

Personally.

Hey, I was the bloke who went out there just after independence when the country was calling for expat expertise to help do a bit of nation building. I met Kenya's first President, the enigmatic Jomo Kenyatta, on several occasions when he opened government and commercial projects that I had designed.

I was recently lectured on the evils of Colonialism by a middle-aged

Australian with a younger African wife. He knew Africa. He had visited several parts of it on business trips, some of many weeks' duration. No, he did not speak any African languages. But he was glad those white supremacists have gone, and Africa is free to govern itself.

He saw not the slightest irony that he was making his comments during a lavish lunch in the comfort and security of an Australian Central Coast garden. We had visited his wife's country last year. There was not a single edible-sized animal in any of their game parks. They had been consumed by a starving population. While their banknotes were worth less than used Kleenex, their President and his wife kept their looted billions of hard currency in western banks.

Fifty-five years ago, I worked with many of the Colonial Civil Service on projects as they handed over to Kenyans. They all followed the rules scrupulously to avoid the dire shame of possibly losing their positions and standing within the community.

But all this strict following of rules and budgets, often overriding common sense, undoubtedly led to some monumental screw-ups. This incident shows the toughness and ingenuity of the early settlers and the ineptitude of some administrators.

To contain cattle and slave raids from Kenya's northern neighbours, the King's African Rifles had posts in the Northern Frontier District. The KAR Colonel planned a new post at the northern end of Lake Turkana. A boat could bring supplies and be used for pursuing the raiders.

In 1923 he ordered a prefabricated boat to be built in Mombasa and looked for someone to lead the expedition.

He found a uniquely qualified 28-year-old naval officer, Commander Maurice Lloyd Vernon who was bored out of his gourd working on his father's farm after minesweeping in World War One.

Arriving in Mombasa, Vernon was aghast to find the boat had been ineptly designed by the harbourmaster. It was 36 feet long, flat bottomed with semi-circular sides. The fundis (skilled workmen) working on it called it the 'sahani' (dish). It was to have two masts with sails of khaki army drill. Vernon pointed out that this shallow keel-less craft would simply blow sideways and make no headway.

"Don't you worry about that," he was reassured. "The harbourmaster has allowed for lee boards. Just like those Dutch chappies."

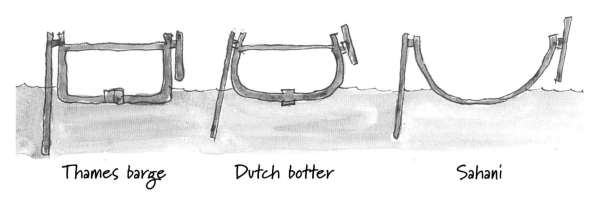

Thames barge   Dutch botter   Sahani

Boats with leeboards need straight sides to brace them, unlike Sahani

The frames and planking were of two-inch teak. The anchor was a trinket, about one tenth of what Vernon considered necessary. He again protested and was told there was no money.

The assembled boat was taken apart by the three Indian carpenters who had built it and loaded onto railway wagons together with rations for the KAR. Vernon also stole a large iron plate from the Public Works Department which he hoped he might be able to use as a keel.

At Thika, everything was loaded onto 14 ox wagons each pulled by 16 animals. With spares, there were over 225 oxen, all of which had to be fed and watered. They travelled about 12 miles a day until the heat became unbearable. To water the animals, they had to dig four feet into dry riverbeds, bail water into canvas-lined troughs dug in the sand from which the herd could drink.

The boat took nearly a month to assemble on site. The planks had dried out and cracked during their desert journey. Vernon immersed them in the lake, steam bent them over a charcoal fire

and crowbarred them into position.

It drew only two inches, and the lee boards hardly met the water. Under sail, it blew sideways and then the lee boards snapped off. Vernon careened the hull and fitted the steel plate as a keel.

With a fair wind they sailed briskly across the lake loaded with vital army stores. In failing light, they struck a sand bar which pushed the iron plate up through the bottom of the boat and it sank in moments. Only three of the 25 aboard could swim. 25 Turkana tribesmen helped to tow the non-swimmers ashore on their backs.

Being careened to fit the metal plate keel

With a fair wind they sailed briskly across the lake, but not for long

The indomitable Vernon and his men salvaged the hull and cargo, removed the plate and repaired the hull. He replaced the broken rudder pintles with planed down hippo teeth! With his now ailing and exhausted crew, they man-hauled this unwieldy craft along the lava-studded shallows. One night, despite burying their charm bracelet anchor in the sand and piling rocks on top of it, it pulled out. *Sahani* was never seen again.

Before I left Kenya I had enough conversational Swahili to ask tribesmen around the country their views comparing the colonial days and post-independence. The results were that the younger generation was in favour, but the older generations missed the honesty and fairness of the old days. "If you went for a job then, you got it on merit, not because of your tribe or by paying a bribe…"

They were united in a common complaint. "In the old days, you saw a few white men driving around in Fords and Austins. Today, you can't cross the road for all these Wabenzi."*

*A derogatory term for a tribe of Mercedes' owners.

JAMES BOND & THE ARMADA

Catholic plots in the 1500s help us fight extremists today

It is over 430 years since the Armada set off. It was not just planned as a land grab to take over England, it was partly a religious war and part family feud. But it became mainly responsible for the creation of the English Secret Service. You thought the Tobermory Galleon blew up by accident? It may have been Q at work...

In 1585, the Spanish grain harvest failed. So what would any good ex-sister-in-law do?

Elizabeth I dispatched a fleet of grain ships to answer the appeal of King Phillip II, King of Spain. After all, he had been married to her half sister Mary for four years until her death at 42 in 1558, probably from uterine cancer. Like many royal marriages, it was not a long courtship. They only met the day before the wedding. Along with many better candidates, Phillip then tried to get Liz, the Virgin Queen, to tie the knot but she wasn't having any of them. (Our History master said she was called the Virgin Queen, but some called her that with err... little conviction.)

In-laws could be a real problem in those days. Phillip took not only the grain but the ships and their crews too.

Except for one.

Primrose was delivering 100 tons of grain to Biscay by unloading into lighters when she was boarded by attackers in armoured doublets. The English seamen fought them before dashing below and shooting upward through the gratings. Ouch, that would hurt. Their attackers fled. Four prisoners were seized and taken back to London.

One of the prisoners was the Governor of Biscay who had led the attack. He was interrogated by the English Secret Service who

The in-laws from hell: Phillip II of Spain and Catherine de Medici

found a letter concealed in a secret pocket ordering the capture of the grain ships to help build up a large armada with ships, troops, slaves and supplies. This letter was traced back to being a direct order from King Phillip.

It is difficult to believe now, but the destination of the planned armada was far from certain. It was thought it might be heading off to the Caribbean to deal with those trespassing Elizabethan privateers. After all, the western half of the globe belonged to Spain; it had been given to them by the Pope. Then it might be to deliver reinforcements for the Duke of Alba who was using a brutal army of 10,000 to bring the Catholic message of love and peace to the Protestant Dutch who had risen against Spanish rule. Then there was talk of Muslims in the eastern Mediterranean wanting to reclaim their lost possessions in Spain. Phillip wasn't short of enemies. Not even counting the in-laws.

In 1573, the 41-year-old Sir Francis Walsingham was Principal Secretary to Queen Elizabeth and charged with protecting her from the very real threat posed by Catholic plots. He immediately set up a secret service that James Bond would recognise today. As in World War Two, he gathered the best brains of Oxford and Cambridge as a sort of Elizabethan Bletchley Park to set up a code and cipher school. There were other specialists that would have delighted the Q who appeared in the films (but was not in the books); invisible inks were the encryptions of the day.

Sir Francis Walsingham's invisible inks would have delighted Q

John Sommers was the expert code breaker, along with Thomas Phelipes who was also a forger. Not only could he produce successful forgeries himself, but he could also detect less successful attempts by others. They decoded Mary Queen of Scots' notes smuggled out of prisons in the bungs of beer barrels quicker than you or I could do *The Times* crossword three across. Anthony Gregory could break open seals and put them back, so you never knew your secret letters had been opened.

Walsingham had a very successful spy in the French Embassy in London and a range of agents across Europe. One source claims that the Armada was put off for a year because Walsingham had persuaded Genoese merchants to be slow payers when paying Spanish accounts.

1587 was not a good year for Spain, Francis Drake had sent fire ships into Cadiz Harbour which not only destroyed 30 ships but their valuable stock of shipbuilding timber. Oh, and he knocked off a treasure galleon on his way home.

Walsingham was a driven man when it came to defending England against Catholic plots. He was Ambassador in Paris in 1572 to witness the St Bartholomew Day's massacre when Catherine de Medici's daughter Margaret, married Henry of Navarre, a Protestant (Hugenot). To spice up the wedding proceedings and to obviate having tiresome in-laws after they had delivered their pressies, Catherine ordered the slaughter of the entire Hugenot guest list. The mob took this as a signal and went off on a bloody rampage which claimed up to 70,000 Hugenot lives.

Walsingham believed that if the Catholic Mary Queen of Scots or Phillip of Spain were to depose Protestant and tolerant Reformation-ist Elizabeth, the same thing could happen in England. The majority was still Catholic. Despite the fact that he was trying to protect the Queen's life, she was always a tightwad and Walsingham funded much of the service from his own pocket which just about cleaned him out.

"It says here 'Light the touch paper and row like hell'"

The Armada sailed in May 1588 with 130 ships, 7,000 sailors and 17,000 soldiers. (Got that? Only one third were sailors.) To make sure of victory, they took more priests than gun aimers. The plan was to pick up an army of 30,000 in the Spanish Netherlands to join in the invasion of England. They would be ferried across in flat-bottomed barges. Oh yes? A couple of other blokes tried this a few centuries later and look how far they got.

After indecisive skirmishes in the Channel, the Spanish were stopped from entering harbour by a blockade of Dutch barges, so they anchored off. This is where Drake pulled out his trusty box of matches and dispatched a small flotilla of fire ships. They did not do so much damage but many of the invaders cut their anchors to clear off in a hurry.

You know the rest of the story. In a year of exceptionally high winds, the Armada was scattered around the coasts of England, Scotland and Ireland. The anchors cut loose in a panic could have saved many from their fates, as they were driven onto lee shores. We get the term Spanish Windlass from the desperate binding of hulls with ropes to try to keep them afloat. As the sailors fell to injury and disease, the soldiers aboard were unable to handle their vessels in a seamanlike manner. Of the 35 ships lost, only one was by English gunfire.

On a recent tour around Scotland, my wife

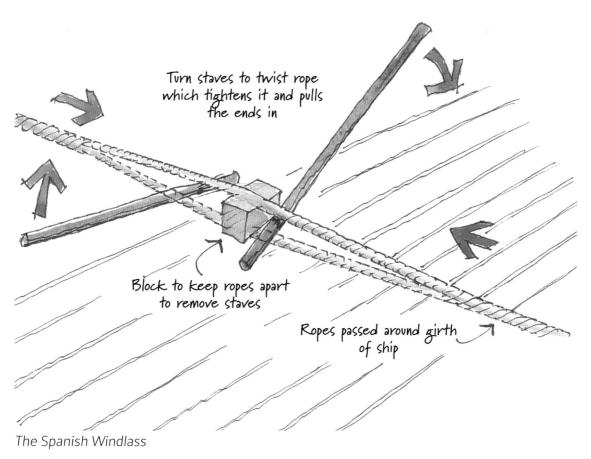

The Spanish Windlass

and I called in at the chocolate-box town of Tobermory on Mull, where the Spanish ship *San Juan de Sicilia* mysteriously blew up. The ship sought shelter, supplies of food and water and facilities to repair the storm-damaged 800-ton merchantman. She was carrying 275 soldiers as well as 26 cannon and two large siege guns.

The local chief of the Macleans agreed to help provided that the troops could be used against the MacDonalds, who had been enemies for generations. Not a problem said Don Diego, the Spanish skipper. But just as security that you bring all my men back, I will take a couple of hostages, including somebody valuable, like your doctor.

In November, the ship suddenly exploded. The fo'c'sle was thrown onto the shore carrying two men with it who survived. One was Maclean's doctor.

The Spanish version was that the ship blew up when gunpowder was being unloaded. We heard a range of alternatives during our stay. One of the most intriguing was that the supplies to the ship were delivered by a local merchant John Smollet from Dumbarton. It was suggested that he was one of Walsingham's agents. He brought aboard a gift of Scottish whisky and, just before leaving, dropped into the hold a piece of 'incendiary lint' which smouldered before bursting into flames. A device said to be developed by Walsingham's boffins. He could have tipped off the doctor to be on the safest part of the ship.

So what do you think? Was this Q at work? Somehow, I like to think so.

"Well that went off as planned, don't you think, doctor?"

SCUPPERED AT SCARPA

If you are going to capture the enemy's fleet, don't let them sink it

21 June marks the anniversary of the deliberate sinking of the captured German Fleet at Scapa Flow in 1919. Quirky looks into the events that led up to this and the subsequent salvage operations.

Recently, my wife and I made several visits to Scotland. We crossed to the Orkneys and learnt how this collection of windswept treeless islands was once the Piccadilly Circus of the Viking world. In Victorian days of Empire, it was said that 'anybody who was anybody' would pass beneath Eros' gaze in Piccadilly. In Viking days, every Thor, Dirk and Hagar would drop into the Orkneys on their way to and from Scandinavia and Greenland.

Britain acquired its vast territorial Empire in many interesting ways, at the end of a sword, cannon or, worst of all, with some smiling smart-arsed

Scarpa Flow, the Piccadilly Circus of the Viking world and during the world wars

lawyer and a proffered quill. The Orkneys joined the real estate portfolio as a wedding present. At 17, the unpleasant and unpopular James III of Scotland was pressured by his cash-strapped family to marry the 15-year-old Scandinavian princess Margaret in 1468, for whom they had negotiated a generous dowry.

However, her father, Christian I of Denmark, Norway and Sweden, was also a bit short of the readies. He could not come up with the agreed 50,000 florins. So he handed over the Orkneys instead. On which James then promptly took out a mortgage. But he could only raise 8,000fl.

These remote islands remained of limited use when Britain's Empire stretched around the globe and the Royal Navy could nip off from bases on the south coast and from her colonies around the world.

Only after the 1871 Franco-Prussian War when a collection of Germanic states became united and referred to the North Sea (the British North Sea) as the German Ocean that the Admiralty brass spluttered into their port and sent the Royal Navy to take over the protected haven of Scarpa Flow as a base.

There were only two sea routes out from Germany: down the Channel, or round the top of Scotland. Scarpa's northerly location gave the Royal Navy easier access to thwart any German ambitions to reach the Atlantic by the northern route.

Scarpa Flow was a natural harbour large enough to take the entire North Sea Fleet and was protected from the brutal semi-Arctic weather, but it was not initially secure against attacks from the newly developed U-boats.

In November 1914, U-18's periscope was spotted by a minesweeper which was the converted wooden 1908 steam trawler Dorothy Gray. She promptly turned and rammed it, damaging the hydroplanes and steering. Out of control, the sub bounced off the bottom and up in front of the trawler who rammed her again. The U-boat again hit the bottom and surfaced to surrender.

A young Dad's Army coast watcher saw this and reported to his superiors. They dismissed it by telling the raw recruit he wouldn't know the difference between a U-boat and a whale.

Scarpa Flow then built defences which protected the fleet from the technology available to U-boats in World War One.

"If it's a whale, then it's got 25 men standing on its back."
(The actual response from the coast watcher when told he couldn't tell a whale from a submarine)

Eventually, just about every large German warship sailed into Scarpa Flow.

But this was no triumphant invasion. After the November 1918 Armistice, the defeated vessels were escorted in by the victors. Proudly heading the port escort column was the Australian Navy's flagship, HMAS Australia in recognition of the country's role in the war.

At the outbreak of hostilities, with the threat of action and potential damage from this 18,000-ton battle cruiser, HMAS *Sydney* and Melbourne panicked the far larger German East Asia Squadron. In a remarkable British intelligence coup, a fake radio message pretended that the Royal Navy had left the Falkland Islands. The Germans seized upon this and hurried there to grab the coal supplies... right into the guns of a vastly superior force which totally annihilated the German Pacific Fleet in December 1914. This disposed of the threat of enemy capital ships in the Pacific and meant that the bulk of the Australian Navy spent the rest of the war in European waters. HMAS *Australia* missed the fleet-shredding Battle of Jutland. She was frequently in dry dock for repairs after several rammings which almost sunk her. No, not the enemy. Well, not really. This time it was by HMS New Zealand.

After the Armistice, the entire German Fleet was seized including 176 of the devastating U-boats, 178 having been lost along with 5,000 men during the war. To put it in perspective, in the first half of 1917, Britain launched 495,000 tons of new ships. In the first quarter, 850,000 were sunk, mainly by U-boats.

The British wanted to destroy the entire German Fleet, being concerned that distributing ships to other navies would upset the balance of power that the Royal Navy enjoyed. They wanted the fleet to be sent to Scapa Flow until their fate could be resolved.

After the mainly indecisive Battle of Jutland, the German Navy was cooped up in port and the Allied blockade reduced German food supplies so much that near starvation rations plus the despondency of defeat gave rise to outbreaks of mutiny in this normally highly disciplined Navy. This was the atmosphere aboard the imprisoned fleet after the war at Scarpa Flow with officers struggling to maintain order on inadequate rations sent from Germany. Concerned that the Allies might distribute the entire fleet among themselves, the senior German officers made plans and gave instructions to cut holes in watertight bulkheads and grease all sea cocks.

At 1000 hours on 21 June 1919, just after the British Battle Squadron left for a torpedo training exercise, Admiral Von Reuter made a signal to all ships to commence the pre-arranged plan.

It was the largest sinking of any day in history.

The Royal Navy was incandescent that the Germans had scuttled their fleet while they were away playing with their torpedoes, but there was also a quiet feeling of satisfaction. Particularly as the French were even more furious, hoping to grab part of the fleet. There was no way now they were going to hand over any of the fleet to their... er bloody Allies. The Royal Navy would continue to reign supreme.

As you saw in I'm sorry, I haven't the foggiest (Chapter 5) the Royal Navy is pretty good at sinking ships, including their own, but had demonstrated that they were out of their depth (sorry) when it comes to salvaging them.

They were quite happy to flog off some of the wrecks to a locally formed salvage group in 1923 which raised four destroyers. There was a glut of scrap metal after World War One and many obsolete ships were going to the breakers anyway, so prices were low. However, Cox and Danks thought 250 pounds for 26 second-hand destroyers, as and where lying, was

"Do you need a wee tow?"
Salvage was achieved by passing cables under the wreck and filling the hulls with air delivered via huge air locks

about market value. They raised them and, when a major coal strike threatened to stop the salvage, they plundered the brimming bunkers of the slightly sunk Seydlitz to finish the job.

The Germans had scuttled their ships by flooding one side, so they keeled over and sank upside down. They thought this would make salvage more difficult.

Not so.

It made it easier to pass cables under the wreck for lifting them and, more importantly, the unarmoured flattish bottoms were uppermost and easier to attach to air locks. These vast cylinders were bolted to the sunken hulls in sections by first making accurate templates which hard-hat divers used to cut holes with an oxyacetylene torch. (Did you know these had been in use since the 19th century?)

The air locks were bolted together by divers in about ten-foot lengths, all underwater, until they were above the high-tide level. Two divers tightened each nut over a compression gasket to make every joint airtight to ten atmospheres. That's skilled workmanship for you. The men then went down the air locks to seal the hulls of the ships. They had decompression chambers at the top for the workers and the divers.

There is so much fascinating detail available online about this remarkable operation. I urge you to check it out. Try Jutland to Junkyard by C S George.

Some of the wrecks are still yielding rare 'low background steel' for radiation sensitive devices such as Geiger counters as there are no radio isotopes in this pre-nuclear age steel.

The remaining seven unsalvaged ships are still paying their way. They are reputed to be some of the most exciting wreck dives on the planet. Well, maybe, but I'm prepared to take their word for it. I feel it is bravely heroic to swim in the creek at Patonga after March. I'll leave this underwater exploration for those creatures that were bred for these conditions. Like the Icelandic shark which has a reported life span of between 250 and 500 years. Sounds great, but they don't reach sexual maturity for 150 years. Such patience. I'd be halfway there.

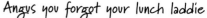

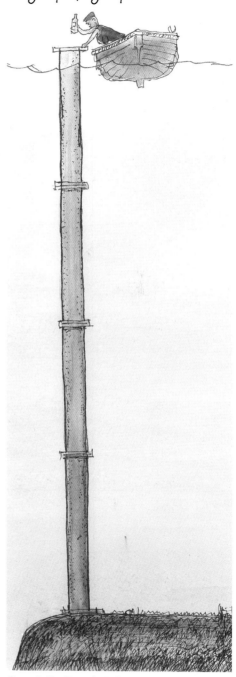

Angus you forgot your lunch laddie

Specially fitted air locks offered access to the hulls

THE FIRST YACHT RACE

We have Charles II to thank for introducing yacht racing to England

Stick with the history lesson, Quirky eventually gets to the subject. We think he chose it because he could draw Nell Gwynn.

"King or not, the windward boat keeps clear"

An American friend and correspondent, who I suspect is a disillusioned Republican, recently remarked how far the UK lags behind the US when it comes to attempting political changes. He lamented that the grand old American tradition of assassinating sitting Presidents, three of the four were Republicans, had sadly lapsed just at a time when he reckoned the country really needed it. And he suggested it should include would-be and ex-Presidents.

Meanwhile, he commented that the UK had only managed to knock off one Prime Minister and one King. Yes, PM Spencer Perceval was shot dead in 1812 by a Liverpool merchant as his government had denied compensation for when the merchant claimed that he was framed for debt by local oligarchs and banged up in a Russian nick. (Would never happen today…) Perceval may have been one of the last honest politicians as he left behind 12 children but only one hundred pounds, five shillings and one penny in the bank.

We all know about the beheading of Charles I, and if we accept the story of Edward II, the cow horn and the red-hot poker at Berkeley Castle in 1327, that would be two Kings. Oliver Cromwell was hanged and beheaded for the regicide of Charles I by his son. However, he had died of natural causes, so he had to be exhumed for the occasion. Does this count?

The 21-year-old Charles II had lost the Battle of Worcester in 1651 and escaped to France in a stumpy collier *Surprise*, pretending, like every other passenger on board, that he was fleeing his creditors. He spent nine years of his twenties in exile on the Continent. From his track record, we can guess how he avoided boredom. While in The Netherlands he also found time to become a skilled and enthusiastic racer in the local 'jachts'.

For his return to England and to the throne in 1660, the city of Amsterdam bought *Mary*, a 50-foot yacht from the East India Company and presented it to the new King and provided an escort of 13 yachts for his arrival.

At 6'2", the tallest King since Henry VII, he was known as the Merry Monarch. Although his plain-ish Portuguese princess wife, Catherine of Braganza, who he met only the day before the wedding to find she spoke no English, was unable to have children, he still found time to sire at least 12 illegitimate ones and proudly introduced them to British society… And still go sailing.

In 27 years, he owned 29 yachts. Anyone that keen on boats can't be all bad.

He sought out and bought *Surprise*, cleaned out the coal dust, refitted her and renamed her *Royal Escape* for day sailing excursions on the Thames.

Mary was traded in for *Katherine*, with a 'K', named after his wife, a larger yacht designed and built by an English shipwright who surprised the doubtful Samuel Pepys by being 'superior in every way'.

The King's brother, the Duke of York, was also impressed and commissioned a near replica, *Anne*. On 1 October 1661 a race was suggested with a prize of one hundred pounds. *Anne* was ahead in the first leg from Greenwich to Gravesend, but passenger Pepys reported that on the return leg, the King took the helm of *Katherine*, demonstrating his skill and winning the first recorded yacht race in England.

As well as a lifelong passion for sailing, Charles developed a strong interest in science, mathematics and navigation. He founded the Royal Observatory at Greenwich in 1665 for the development of navigation.

Charles was an early riser; leaving whoever's bed it was to go sailing at 5:00am. Sometimes day sails would turn into sleepovers. Pepys reports rowing over to a Dutch merchantman and buying three large cheeses at 4d each and oysters from local fishermen before dossing down on acres of silken cushions.

When cruising with friends, the King's yachts would be attended by a galley galley – wouldn't that be good? Outsourcing all the cooking and washing up to a tender?

My abbreviated version of Pepys' Diaries does not record the King's favourite favourite, Nell Gwynn as being aboard the yachts, but he knew her well: "Pretty, witty Nell." Perhaps not as well as Charles as she bore him two sons in 1670 and 1671.

We seem to think of her with a basket of oranges clasped to her bosom. (They were sold at 6d each in theatres when the daily wage was 10d.) Yes, she started off as an orange seller but became a popular and talented actress in the restoration comedy. Remember that the puritanical Cromwell, like the Taliban and too many others today, had closed theatres and places of entertainment as being instruments of the devil. This fresh

"I would like two oranges please"

surge in showbiz brought a new word into the English vocabulary: actress. Up until then, female roles had been played by blokes in drag.

With no vowels in her surname, you can guess Nell was Welsh and she was proud of… er… getting around a bit. As a result, she enjoyed a wealthy lifestyle.

She once found her coachman involved in a fight with another who had referred to his employer as a whore. Nell stepped in.

"Of course I am. Now find something else to fight about."

Meanwhile, back on the Thames, Charles continued to race his fleet and enjoy cruising and day sails, often accompanied by Pepys for the next quarter of a century. This encouraged others with access to enough taxpayers' money to build and race yachts. But you wonder how they got on before the advent of the racing rules. I mean, you couldn't just pop down to the chandlery and check about who had right of way at the windward mark in *Rules in Practice*, could you?

But don't forget, Charles was King.

And look at those gun ports.

Would you make a protest against a King armed with six pounders?

The racing rules may have got a bit more sophisticated

WHATEVER HAPPENED TO DIESEL?

On his way to help the British Navy – did he jump or was he pushed?

Until recently we all thought of diesels as heavy clunkers but economical and reliable... Did you know that over 90 years ago they powered the world's largest land planes because of their fuel efficiency? Hard to imagine taking off with a couple of Gardeners under the wings, isn't it?

Here's how it started.

Straight 6 outboard engines   V-12 inboard engines   First class passengers in the nose   Business class in the wings between engines   Double decker fuselarge for other passengers

90 years ago, the largest aircraft in the world was diesel powered

Anyone who has one of these engines in their boat has several reasons to be grateful to Herr Rudolf Christian Diesel.

Back in my day, before diesels became lighter, more compact and affordable, boat owners were stuck with a petrol engine marinating in the bilgewater. Not only were you carrying an explosive fuel which could blow you and your boat sky high or just burn it to the waterline, a sad event I once witnessed. You were also heavily dependent on an electrical ignition system with fabric insulation that for most British installations were made by a firm that called their automotive products 'King of the Road' which we referred to in Chapter 10 – many frustrated customers referred to them as 'The Prince of Darkness'.

The first petrol engine was created by Nicholas Otto in 1876 with a spark plug igniting an air / petrol mix in a fairly low compression ratio. It showed a thermal efficiency of 20%, or double that of a steam engine. Herr Rudolf Christian Diesel thought he could do better.

Diesel was actually born in Paris to a German family who struggled to make a living with their leather workshop. Young Rudy worked in the family business and made deliveries on a hand cart while also attending school.

Every so often, the Germans feel the need to start a war with someone. In 1870, it was the turn of the French, which forced the family to move to London. Whiz-kid Rudy was later sent to stay with an uncle in Augsburg who taught mathematics. Under his tutorship, he rose to top of the class at the Royal Bavarian Poly. He took a gap year working in Switzerland before returning to Paris to set up a refrigeration company with his old professor.

He was head-hunted back to Germany to lead the R & D for a major engineering firm. He was given the handy moniker of therodynamilforssdirecktorgeneral. (You wonder if the Germans get by with a standard sized Scrabble board or if they need one of

"Triple word score Otto; that's 2,616 points"

their own.)

Rudy soon found out, as many of us have, that all your creations belong to your employer while you are in their service. He was testing high pressure engines using ammonia as a fuel when an explosion put him in hospital with lifelong health and eyesight problems. However, the contacts he made in Switzerland recognised his work and helped with funding his experiments.

Twenty-one years after the first petrol engine, Rudy unveiled his first compression ignition engine. You can still see it in the Munich Technical Museum. He claimed the efficiency was greater than that of the petrol engine because, without a spark plug, it relied on the fuel to explode from the heat generated by a higher pressure. This used more of the heat energy which was converted into more power than a petrol one which relied on an ignition system. A diesel had to use about a 20:1 compression ratio for

Thirty years later, diesels were powering aircraft

the fuel to ignite on its own, whereas a petrol engine at the time, say in the Rolls Royce Silver Ghost, was a measly 3.2:1.

The diesel engine was slower revving and had to be of much stronger and heavier construction. However, it showed an efficiency of 26.2%.

The new engine was appreciated by many who used steam engines in industrial plants and by ship owners. Not only for its efficiency but also because its fuel could be supplied from gravity-fed header tanks rather than a bunch of blokes with shovels. Imagine how much easier this would have made refuelling at sea.

However, many say that Rudy pushed his engine onto the market before it was fully developed which resulted in some of his early customers finding them unreliable and demanding a refund. This slid him into a mental breakdown and, some say, a financial hole from which he found it hard to claw his way out despite the royalties from the growing acceptance of his engines. We'll come to that later.

In 1904 the French started using his diesel engines in their submarines when the popular propulsion up to then was, amazingly, steam!

The British only started with subs in 1900 and persisted with steam power despite Jacky Fisher, the father of the Dreadnought and the modern Navy declaring "The most fatal error ever imaginable is to put steam engines in submarines." However, he was not First Sea Lord at the time and was out voted.

Others supported Fisher and planned to develop the use of diesel engines in a new range of subs. So Herr Diesel was asked to come to England to discuss it. The German Navy was using his engines in their U-boats but wanted exclusive rights. He refused.

The world was recognising the huge potential of the new engine in their most important industries. He had sold the US patents to Anheuser Busch who wanted it for their breweries. The British Government wanted it for their Navy.

On 29 September 1913, Rudy packed his bags and hopped aboard the steamer *Dresden* at Antwerp heading for Harwich.

After dinner, he asked for a wake-up call at 6:15am and retired to his cabin. His night gear was later found laid out on the bed, but it had not been slept in and there was no sign of Herr D, except for an overcoat neatly folded on deck. Why would you take that off if you were planning to jump into the North Sea in September? It's cold in there.

His body was found a week later by a small Dutch boat that emptied the pockets but left the decomposing corpse in the water.

He had supposedly made millions from royalties, but his bank accounts had been emptied. Before leaving, he had given his wife a suitcase to be opened a week later. Some reports say this contained over a million dollars; others quote 20,000DM which was 15 years of a skilled workers salary at the time. An agreement with the British Royal Navy could have brought in substantial royalties and that cash could have kept them going until he had a deal.

So you can understand why some suspect foul play. I think we can dismiss the shovel makers, but some think Big Coal was concerned about the rise of demand for oil. All this was 11 months before the Germans started another war in which diesel-powered U-boats were part of their plan to starve Britain into defeat. So they wouldn't want them to leave the steam age and go over to diesel would they?

I hope someone from Netflix reads this. I would like to see it as a drama series.

NAPOLEON'S AUSTRALIA

Could New Holland have become New France?

Suppose for a moment, just suppose, that the following events had happened.

That the 18-year-old Austrian-born art student had shown sufficient talent to be admitted to the prestigious Vienna Academy of Fine Arts and not been rejected in October 1907...

What if Leopold Loijka, the driver of a 1911 Graff & Stiff 28 / 32 double phaeton sports model had not mistakenly turned right on Franz Joseph Street and stopped in front of Schiller's delicatessen to back up...

And if Jean-François de La Pérouse, when fitting out his ships *L'Astrolabe* and *La Boussole* for a four-year voyage of discovery had not been so selective about the hordes of volunteers who flocked to sign on. What if he had taken on the 5'7" 16-year-old Italian kid who had just graduated from the Paris Ecole Militaire in October 1785 but was unsure if he wanted to join the Army or the Navy? He showed some talent in mathematics and gunnery which he thought would be more valued by the Navy. La Pérouse turned him down.

Napoleon failed to make the short list

If these events had turned out differently, Hitler might have become an artist or even an architect. (They thought he showed slightly more talent here than his drawing.) Emperor Franz Joseph and his wife Sophia would not have been outside the deli where Garrilo Princip, the sixth Serbian assassin was standing, with a loaded revolver, wondering why the other killers had failed or given up. There would have been no world wars and Napoleon would have disappeared into the Pacific in 1788. The remains of one of La Pérouse's ships was not found until 2005.

Not only would millions upon millions of lives had been saved; the world would be a very different place.

Did you know, for example, that Port Jackson was being prepared as a base from which the British (who had their paint box out and wanted to add a bit more pink to the atlas) intended to drive the Spanish out of South America? They wanted to make it like Australia or New Zealand instead of a hotch-potch of Spanish and Portuguese colonies that would squabble for the next 200 years. Then Napoleon came along, and they had to make friends with their second favourite enemy (Spain) to go up against their traditional one of the last 500 years.

I have just been captivated by Terry Smyth's brilliantly researched book *Napoleon's Australia*. Checking history in France for this period is not easy. In November 1981 I racked up to their Musee National de la Marine with my hulking ex-US Navy and square-rigger trained boss and we asked to see their exhibits on Trafalgar, just to get their take on the naval battle that changed Europe. "S'il vous plait."

Trafalgar? Beaucoup de head scratching and Gallic shrugs. "Je ne sais pas." Never happened, mate.

Napoleon's enthusiasm for the great southern continent did not waver after failing to make La Perouse's short list. (Sorry.)

He was actually slightly above average height for the time. Certainly taller than Nelson. The British PR machine tried to diminish his threat by diminishing his stature. His passion for Australasia increased. Mainly because of his passion for Marie Josèphe Rose de Tascher de La Pagerie.

"Just call me Joséphine."

Interesting how the big N met Joséphine. She was the mistress of his best friend. She used to organise parties and soirees for him. It was said that invitations to these were particularly sought after. She would sometimes show up naked.

So, on seeing Joséphine like this, several thoughts probably ran under Napoleon's voluminous hat... We can skip the first few but, as an afterthought, he probably imagined that she would not cost a fortune in her dress allowance.

"This lady is not going to need an expensive dress allowance"

Dream on buddy. She became just about the most expensive hobby in history.

He was utterly besotted with this Martinique-born widow whose husband was guillotined during The Terror on the Stalinist charge of 'not showing enough remorse for losing a battle'. Pour encourager les autres? Living on a sugar-rich diet in the West Indies it is reported she had the same feature as Elizabeth I: blackened teeth. This was considered a status symbol by those able to afford this highly priced luxury.

Six years older than him, Napoleon churned out voluminous daily Mills-&-Boon letters to her while he was on manoeuvres or slaughtering Europe a piece at a time. His handwriting was so bad that he often could not read it himself and dictated to a series of blushing scribes. You can find some of the letters online. How would you fancy dictating that you have the Austrian Army trapped in a wood and will wipe them out tomorrow after breakfast... "But I would rather be in your little

Napoleon dictates a French letter to a blushing clerk

forest of delight..."

She barely deigned to reply unless it was with a shopping list of plants and animals for 'Malmaison', the dilapidated renovator's dream she instructed him to buy.

With her flair, and his loot from plundering Europe, the place would top any House & Garden list of the period. Then she wanted enough wild animals to stock a zoo. And not just from Europe. "No more presents from the seaside or spotted stoats from southern Slovenia. Get me some exotic stuff. I want things from the Caribbean, Asia and New Holland." (That's what it was until the Admiralty changed the name to Australia.) "Some kangaroos and black swans for a start."

During the Napoleonic Wars, expedition ships collecting fauna and flora were given free passage by either side in the name of science. But getting foreign plants back home still with leaves on, or livestock with a pulse wasn't easy then. It still isn't if you are a sheep. But one captain had a good track record here. Nicholas Thomas Baudin was the David Attenborough of his day at finding rare species and, like Frank Buck, would 'Bring 'em back alive'.

In 1800 he set off with two ships, Le Geographe and Le Naturalist on voyage during which he was instructed to stock up Josephine's garden and zoo.

Other members of his crew were given different orders. How easy would it be to take over Port Jackson and from there, the rest of New Holland? Dead easy in fact, not only was it lightly protected; the French would have a ready-made militia at their disposal on arrival. Who? Well, the British had transported over 800 able-bodied Irish, many on political charges. They had to be fit, they were there to work. That's more than the standing army guarding the place. Just like the Luftwaffe in

"You've been upgraded to First Class. You are moving in with the kangaroos."

World War Two*, the French knew they could count on the Irish in any struggle against the British.

Terry Smyth paints a vivid picture of how this might have come to pass and how only extraordinary luck prevented it. He tells history like our two superb History masters who gave many of us an enduring passion for it, even six decades after leaving school… History was not just a series of dates but an ongoing soap opera, driven by the personalities of the time. I'm not going to tell you any details because I want you to read his book, be entertained and be astonished at just how fortunate Australia was.

---

*If you look for 'IRA in the blitz' you might find the bomb they planted in Coventry, nine days before World War Two started which killed five people. History tells us that the IRA campaign to bomb British cities ended in March 1940. Not quite. They coordinated with the Germans putting bombs in places where the public would gather during air raids, like hospitals and air raid shelters. They used phosphorous-based incendiary devices because you could not extinguish them with water. That is why we spent the war surrounded by galvanized buckets of sand from which I had to be restrained from making sand pies. Many Irish were rounded up in the Midlands and interned on the Isle of Man. My father was part of a police team that removed these bombs. After his funeral, my brother-in-law had to get the bomb squad to remove the souvenirs from his workshop.

THE END RESULT

It's not only harbours that rot ships

It was love at first sight.

It was also my first holiday and view of the sea, although some may say the muddy turbulence of the Bristol Channel hardly qualified. Just after the war, we left the bombed-out rubble of Birmingham for a week and toured the coastal attractions from Minehead to the Torridge Estuary. I cannot recall where I saw *Result*, but it was probably Appledore or Bideford.

It is the sheer sheer of her that grabs your attention. It swoops from an elegant elliptical counter down low amidships before soaring up to that bowsprit that continues the line 20 feet beyond her elegant clipper bow. And look at that yacht-like underbody.

A slightly romantic view of my first sighting. The hull was all matt coal-sack black with grey bulwarks and there were no top masts or square sail yards. The lighter coloured bottom shows the yacht-like lines

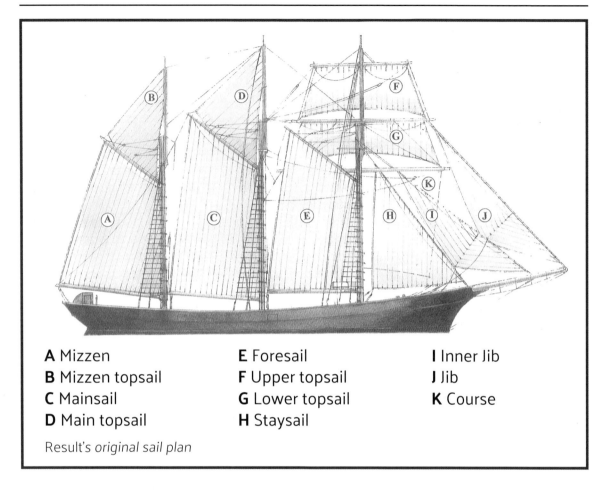

A Mizzen
B Mizzen topsail
C Mainsail
D Main topsail

E Foresail
F Upper topsail
G Lower topsail
H Staysail

I Inner Jib
J Jib
K Course

Result's original sail plan

She had just had a re-fit as Britain had lost a vast number of ships during the war. This included a 120hp diesel and the topmasts had been taken down, but the three lower masts ones remained proudly aloft.

"Hey mister, is this a real live pirate ship?" I must have had the look of a boating tragic even then because the crew member invited me to trudge the hill of her deck as it rose up to that flaring bow and I recall the tailored Victorian elegance of the horseshoe sofa in the skipper's quarters. One of the original owners was a joiner.

In 1892, the schooner owner and keen yachtsman, Thomas Ashburner, flush with years of profitability from the family's fleet, decided to add one more to show that sailing vessels could still compete with steam. They cost less and had greater cargo capacity in hulls that were free from engine rooms and coal bunkers. Some showed a 25% return in their first year.

An iron-hulled three-masted topsail schooner was designed by his brother Richard, Captain Wright and her future commander and Paul Rogers, a shipbuilder in Carrick Fergus, Northern Ireland. She had to be fast, handled by a small crew with a shallow draft and be able to sail without ballast. Oh, and she had to be beautiful. Does that sheer line look like a commercial vessel to you, or one ordered by a yachtsman? She was built from the best quality Low Moore iron from Yorkshire, prized for its strength and resistance to corrosion. The high specification unfortunately, just like *Cutty Sark* 27 years earlier, sent her builder broke.

She was a successful coastal trader for the Ashburners until they sold their fleet in 1909 and she was acquired by a consortium of six owners. In 1914 she was fitted with a 45hp Dutch Kromhout engine.

The Germans decimated the British sailing ship fleet in World War One by sinking over 200 of them. The Navy requisitioned a number of them as Q-ships, including *Result*. These pretended to be merchant ships on which the U-boats would not waste a valuable torpedo but surface and destroy then with gunfire. A fake crew would take to the lifeboat and, when within range, hidden guns on the schooners would pound the U-boat.

Result was in action three times, but she was badly damaged in April 1917 by U-45 but managed to score a hit on the conning tower.

The second in command at this time was Lt G H P Muhlhauser RN, despite his Teutonic moniker; he was the first Englishman to sail around the world in his own yacht, the 62-foot *Amaryllis* from 1920 to 1923. I devoured his book during schooldays.

After regaining her full rig to star in Carol Reed's *Outcast of the Islands*, *Result* was reduced to a two-masted motor-sailer in 1950 which is how I remember her in later meetings.

In Ilfracombe in 1957 she was together with her timber contemporary *Kathleen and May*. During our Channel cruises of the mid-sixties, we saw her when she delivered coal to Alderney. She was shabby and down-at-heel, her complexion battered by her 70 years of knocking around some rough waterfronts.

In 1969, I was on leave from east Africa in North Devon. She was aground in the Torridge Estuary, her last owner had died and she was put up for sale. I got to wondering what would happen if four young guys of my age got together and bought her. Then I went back to building game lodges in Africa and later on being sent around the world

The sort of escapist adventure yarn I enjoy reading

by my New York employer. Some of the experiences and people I met in those years gave me the inspiration to use a fictional *Result* as the basis for writing and illustrating the sort of escapist sailing adventure yarn that I enjoy reading. Ordinary people up against extraordinary situations. Written in the same style as this book. You may even get a chance to read it before long.

Sadly, instead of my romantic fictional fate, she suffered a cruel blow. While the more fragile, timber *Kathleen and May* had numerous rebuilds since the seventies and is now in survey and giving joy to thousands on her Irish Sea cruises, *Result* was acquired by a museum whose way of honouring this noble vessel was to remove the masts, put her ashore and throw a tarpaulin over the hull, hiding the sweep of that deck. The museum did not respond to questions about the condition of those wonderful Victorian quarters shoehorned into her stern.

When the 1874 three-masted iron-barquentine *James Craig* was rescued by a group of enthusiasts from a Tasmanian creek 40 years ago, she was reported to have had over a thousand holes in her iron hull. My great great grandfather was a riveter then with Bartram and Haswell who built her. But he did a lousy job as 40% of the plates had to be replaced 108 years later. She is now a glorious sight of Australia's east coast giving

Result *under her tarpaulin. You can still admire the lines, but not much else. Compare this with* Constitution *on Page 51 or the* James Craig

immense pleasure to those on board and the rest of us who just look at her.

Result arrived at the museum on her own bottom. If she had been rescued by enthusiasts with the same dedication to restoring and finding funds for this wonderful ship with her iron hull that came with an almost lifetime guarantee, she would now be bringing excitement and thrills to all of us with a chance to sail aboard this magnificent pinnacle of sailing ship design. And after hearing of Russian subs sniffing around the Irish coast as I write, maybe she could notch up another conning tower.

Result battling with submarines once again

RUSSIAN ROULETTE

We should learn lessons from history

It was late April and I was editing this manuscript when the editor asked if I could add a story reflecting on the current Russia-Ukraine crisis. This is meant to be a humour book and it is hard to find levity in the psychopathic genocide being carried out as I write this. However, a similar situation has happened before. Let's see if the results will be similar.

The Russian flagship, a 15,000-ton Kniaz Suvorov, leading the fleet using 1.8 tons of coal a mile. You don't many miles per gallon out of a battle fleet

Back in the 1900s, Russia and Japan looked upon Asia the way that the European powers had regarded Africa: a backward place that needed civilising and the introduction of a firm hand to bring it into the 20th century.

Russia wanted a year-round ice-free port in the east. Japan wanted Korea and the same bits of Manchuria as the Ruskies. So they declared war on Russia.

In the Japanese tradition of attacking before actually declaring war (which they repeated in 1941), they launched a surprise raid on the Russian Pacific Fleet in Port Arthur on 9 February 1904. Torpedo boats sneaked in to damage the two heaviest battleships and a cruiser. The defending shore batteries kept the Japanese from inflicting further damage, so they blockaded the port.

The psychological hit was devastating.

Who was this tiny nation of small people to challenge the might of Imperial Russia? But wait, it gets worse. The Japanese then landed a military force, set up artillery hidden behind the surrounding hills and sank just about the entire Russian Pacific Fleet. A few ships escaped only to run into Japanese mines. The Russian defenders surrendered. An Army sinking a Navy? I think this is a first for the history books.

With the Pacific Fleet wiped out, the Russians would have to use their other one, the Baltic Fleet. That one on the other side of the world.

The bloke in charge of it had the handy moniker of Admiral Zinovi Petrovich Rozhdestvenski. He reviewed the ships available for this voyage and picked a batch of 42 battleships, cruisers and destroyers. A fortune had been spent on modernising the Navy and he chose what he considered to be the modern pick of the fleet. After all, only one of them carried sails. He rejected all the other entries as being worthless scrap metal.

All he had to do now was get them 18,000 miles (33,000km) to the east coast. And to arrange for fuel and supplies along the way. I don't know what this is in miles per gallon but his own 15,000-ton flagship, *Kniaz Suvorov*, cruised at 10 knots using 1.8 tons of coal per mile and had bunkers for 1,350 tons.

Just to complicate things, as a fleet at war, it was not allowed to be supplied at any port. His brand-new battleship was unusually built in the capital St Petersburg. Most of the Russian Navy came from Ukraine which was their equivalent of Britain's Clydeside.

As they set off down the Baltic, Russian propaganda and intelligence showed that it has changed little in 118 years. One ship reported it had been attacked by Japanese torpedo boats. Her fearless compatriots gathered round and fired wildly at the enemy. The nearest Japanese warship was on the other side of the globe. They had attacked a hapless British herring drifter. Two were killed and every other member of the crew was injured. Britain, with the world's largest Navy, was incensed and for a while there was a real threat of war until Russia made a grovelling apology.

The first refueling was in Spain. When you want to do anything against the interests of Britain and the rest of the world, you can always count on the Germans. The America Hamburg line was there to top up fleet's bunkers. At the next stop, Dakar, the fleet ignored the International Waters rule and just pulled up to the dock and aimed their guns at the town.

Refueling the fleet must have been a pleasant occupation. It was 39 degrees at the time and the coal had to be shovelled into canvas bags, carried from the storage yards

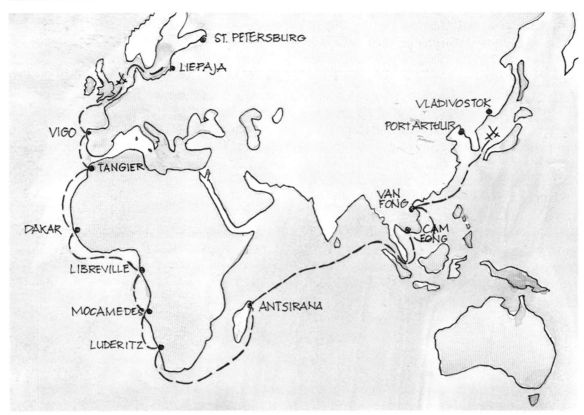

When your country is so big, you have to sail halfway around the world to get from one side to the other

to the bunkers, emptied, and start all over again. Thousands and thousands of tons. By the bagful. Even the disciplined and highly efficient Royal Navy could only manage between 20 and 75 tons an hour at the time. You can see why Jacky Fisher and the civilian First Sea Lord, Winston Churchill, converted the fleet to oil just before World War One…

The sailors in Dakar could only work for 20 minutes in these conditions using cotton waste between their teeth against the coal dust which permeated every part of the ships.

Like a relay race around the world via coaling stations, after seven months the Baltic Fleet arrived on the eastern coast only to be told to wait until they could be joined by

reinforcements. Reinforcements? The ships that the Admiral rejected did not go to the scrapyard. They were wheezing their weary way around a third of the planet to support him. The original 42 ships were joined by the 52 others on 9 May. Wow! A total of 94 ships. The Japanese won't have a chance.

Admiral Zinovi had made sure that he had plenty of coal when he went into battle. He overloaded his ship with 1,700 tons of it. He stowed it everywhere, particularly on deck. This pushed his top-heavy ship down in the water by 4'6" lowering the effectiveness of the armour plating…

The 94-strong Russian Armada was met by Admiral Togo Heihachiro with his smaller fleet

125

of mainly modern British-built ships. Britain was also supplying intelligence sourced from Russian cable traffic. Togo and many other officers had trained in the UK, originally intending to attend The Royal Naval College at Dartmouth. However, just after he arrived, the Admiralty decided that no places were to be made available to Japanese cadets; he was sent to HMS *Worcester*, a training ship in Greenhithe. He became a great fan of Nelson and believed that he was the reincarnation of the great man. He used his manoeuvres of exactly 100 years ago at Trafalgar to cross the Russian Fleet.

He shelled the flagship, precisely knocking out the steering station which started a fire, injured the Admiral and several other officers. Then he popped a few torpedoes above the now submerged armour of the Admiral's flagship. Showing their usual compassion for their own servicemen, 20 wounded officers were saved by a destroyer, including the Admiral, leaving a young midshipman at the emergency helm. He and all the 927 others were lost when their flagship rolled over and sank shortly afterwards. Then Togo set about destroying half of the Russian Fleet.

But the oblivious Tsar Nick was not interested in peace talks. He had only lost three quarters of his fleet and thousands of casualties. But he had millions more in his vast population to replace them. Nor were the Japanese, who were enjoying a string of victories with their superior tactics, weapons and intelligence. Until they realised that they

Starvation rations for the military – complain and you were ordered to be shot

were running out of resources. The Japanese eventually asked President Teddy Roosevelt to broker a peace. This was signed at the Treaty of Portsmouth, New Hampshire and Teddy won the Nobel Peace prize for his negotiating skills.

Russia was unable to pay the reparations demanded by the Treaty as it was flat broke and heavily indebted to foreign lenders. These debts were later repudiated which made Russia the pariah of the industrial and financial world.

Trotsky wrote in his book *1905* that 80% of the Russian population was peasant farmers who were taxed to death to provide funds for railways, military supplies and equipment and modernising the Navy. (In 1904 only one had sails remember.) These funds had been siphoned off by a favoured few for high style luxurious western living.

Military rations were sold so that in June 1905, the crew of the battleship *P o t e m k i n ** mutinied at the starvation rations and putrefied meat. Their kindly understanding captain listened to their grievances and ordered them

to be shot. The firing squad was on the same rations and refused to do this and the revolution began.

The revolution was to end corrupt government by a few crooks that plundered state coffers from an already destitute land with massive debts. They also treated their armed forces with contempt and withheld modernisation and adequate supplies.

So many were glad that the revolution occurred when it did. These wrongs could never happen again, could they?

It seems to me that Russian leaders are consumed by the perceived grievances of history but fail to learn from it.

We must not make the same mistake.

Macron offers Putin a way out:
"Would you like to borrow our white flag?"

---

* See Eisenstein's 1925 film which is still gripping.

Illustrated by John Quirk

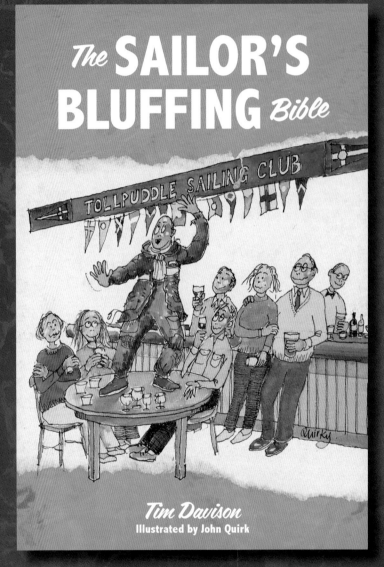

Learn how to bluff with the best in the sailing club bar and manoeuvre yourself onto sleek yachts and fast dinghies. Once there, our tips on what to do, what to wear and what to say will come in very handy. You may even be asked back!

To find out more visit www.fernhurstbooks.com